When the Wind Chimes Chime

When the Wind Chimes Chime

Ending the Greatest Fear of All

DONNA CORSO

Foreword by Neale Donald Walsch

To order additional copies of this book, contact:
Xlibris Corporation
1-888-795-4274
www.Xlibris.com
Orders@Xlibris.com

FOREWORD

by Neale Donald Walsch

You are going to be very, very glad that you read this book.

I don't know what else I could say that would make this foreword more compelling. *You are going to be very, very glad that you read this book.*

First, because it is extraordinarily well written. Second, because its subject is compelling. Third, because its treatment of the subject is spellbinding. But finally, and most important of all, because I believe your soul has *called* you to these pages.

If you are not already aware, this book is about death. Not always a welcome or exciting subject. Yet this book's author, Donna Corso, leads us into an exploration of this topic in a way that removes fear completely from our contemplations of it. That is not a small thing, that is not a little gift. And that is why your soul brought you here—to remove fear from any thoughts you have, any notions or ideas you have about death.

It has been a long time since a book brought a lump to my throat, a tear to my eye, a huge smile to my heart, and an explosion of love to my soul all at the same time. I experienced being embraced by a silent joy here, a feeling of reunion and reconnection with the deeper part of myself that knows—and *knows* that it knows—all there really *is* to know about life and death and the mysteries of the whole process that we call the Journey of the Soul. Yet while the feeling of knowing all of this came over me, it felt so good, so comforting, so expanding and enlarging to be reminded of it all again. To have my highest hopes and my grandest thoughts affirmed.

And the marvelous thing about *When the Wind Chimes Chime* is that it does not talk *at* you, but *with* you. We're invited to explore many questions here, for the author has done a marvelous job of placing before us items for deeper reflection, thus expanding the book's reach from her mind to our own. I love a book that drives me back into my own mind, allowing me to not only receive the author's wisdom but to retrieve my own.

I don't want to tell you much about the specifics of what is found here. That would spoil it for you. I simply want to encourage you with every fiber of my being to absorb what is offered for you between these pages because when you have done that, I am *sure* that you will say, "Oh my, what a *wonderful* book!" And I know that you will find 101 other people to pass it on to.

Thank you, Donna, for this remarkable read and this helpful treasure. I shall share it with everyone!

The Soul Plan

It was long, long ago
in that timeless, spaceless forever-world between lifetimes
that a group of souls came together
to set their future into motion

The Plan was designed
agreements were reached
and a new mission was set forth

He rested at the edge of a crystalline stream that sleepily meandered its way through a lush meadow, thick carpeted with poppies, daffodils, and lavender— all dressed in hues so brilliant that earthly eyes would be blinded by the sight. But here, in this in-between world, were colors that human eyes could not behold, fragrances that humans could scarcely imagine. Candescent-feathered birds filled the misty air with their heavenly symphonies. And the soft, warm breeze carried a distant melody of wind chimes in its wispy tendrils .

He was not really a "he" nor a "she" nor an "it," but a soul—a golden-colored spark of divine essence of some unseen source-of-all-that-is.

How long had it been? How long since that last earth experience had ended? How long had he been resting and dreaming and visioning his next adventure? A day? A year? A millennium? It was hard to judge time when suspended in a void of timelessness.

He felt so refreshed, so gloriously revitalized! Yet something tugged at him ... a sense of yearning, of purpose yet to be fulfilled. He pondered the possibilities. What would be the theme of his next lifetime? What could he accomplish? His soul-heart yearned to make a difference in his next incarnation, especially a difference in the lives of children.

Oh, how he had loved children! In previous lifetimes, he had observed many misfortunes among the little ones—cruelties, sicknesses, dysfunctions of all kinds. And though he understood that those sad occurrences had been part of a bigger plan, even so, he vowed that one day he would help them. He would embrace them, he would comfort them, he would remind them of their beauty and their wonder and their power. His soul-heart leaped with joy, just thinking about how much love he could lavish on the children. Yes! That would be his purpose ... next time.

As he sat dreaming of what he could do for the earth children, he began to sense a soft presence drawing near, attracted to his soul-thoughts. At first, he only felt it—a slight stirring of the energy surrounding him, like butterfly wings gently brushing his aura. Soon, he began to see with his soul-eyes a swirling mass of deep indigo coming closer and closer. It felt comfortable, warm, loving, and wise; and gradually, it began to take form. He recognized it as a part of his soul family. They had been journeying together through thousands of incarnations. He joyously welcomed the indigo presence to come sit next to him.

They began a soul-to-soul communion, a conversation that seemed to flow silently between them in a universal language that needed no sound.

And the Soul Plan began to emerge...

Having expressed a deep desire to go back and make a difference in the lives of many children, the two souls discussed the details of the Soul Plan. By this time, several other souls had gathered near, wanting to be part of it, and the stage was set, the agreements made, the roles selected. Joyously, they merged back into one oversoul to await the time for the Soul Plan to unfold.

It seemed only an instant... or perhaps a millennium.

It began in the earth time of February 1961, when the golden soul located the appropriate vehicle for his earth journey. He was born a male, and his new earth parents named him Gordy. Life was good—a typical earth life with all the joys and sorrows, the ups and downs of human life. Time passed. It was the summer of 1987 that he recognized another member of his soul group—a beautiful woman named Joey. Their eyes met. Their hearts remembered. They fell in love, and in accordance with the Soul Plan, they married.

Three years later, another member of their soul group arrived. Gordy and Joey were thrilled to welcome him—their first son, and they named him Joshua. Cradling his new little son in his arms, Gordy vaguely remembered a "dream" he had had about helping children. He had come to see so many dysfunctions among the children even in this lifetime, and he wondered how he could help them to become the human beings they were meant to be. He had an idea. He would create a tool that would help children remember who they are—beautiful, powerful, unlimited beings.

Four years passed, and soon, another member of their soul group was felt hovering around them. It would be nine months after a special vacation that this soul would enter the world as their second son. They named him Andraez. It was clear from the moment he arrived that he was a very old soul. His sparkling emerald eyes held a depth of wisdom, and his aura hinted of indigo, though few could see it and fewer still would grasp its meaning.

The first time Gordy's and Andraez's eyes met, just moments after birth, there was an unspoken recognition, and a communion took place on a level that was beyond their human comprehension. With their silent gaze, they reminded each other of the Soul Plan.

Thirteen months later, the final member of the soul group arrived, and they named him Zachary. Their family was complete. Their journey together through life was good.

It was a happy time … and then …

Part One

THE STORY OF ANDRAEZ

Chapter One

"Turn off my lungs," he whispered weakly as he struggled to tug the oxygen mask from his face with a subtle but clear urgency.

Startled parents responded in unison. Gordy hurried around to the side of the bed to replace the breathing apparatus over his son's mouth. As he attempted to reposition the mask, Andraez grabbed his wrist and, mustering the last of his waning strength, pushed the hand and the mask away from him. Looking directly into his daddy's eyes, he repeated softly yet firmly, "Turn off my lungs."

Those eyes of his! Those deep green pools of mystery and magic that penetrated right through you, touching your soul. Gordy understood. He knew the time had come, the time they all had dreaded, time to let go of this wondrous child who had brightened their world for seven years.

The dark, suffocating heaviness that had hung in the air for days weighed even heavier. Hisses and beeps of medical equipment joined with the acrid aroma of an intensive care unit where hurried footsteps had brought more poking, prodding, recording.

Now … time was standing still … time was running out. With an anguished sigh of release, Gordy's wrist went limp as he helplessly witnessed Andraez take charge of his own final moments.

Through tear-flooded eyes, Gordy managed to smile at his child and began to talk to him gently, encouragingly, thanking him for his beautiful presence in their lives over the past seven years. They had learned so much from this wise little soul. He had been their teacher.

Together, he and Andraez had prepared for this moment. As a certified hypnotherapist, Gordy had guided his son on many a visualization where Andraez could journey over to the "other side" and see all the beings of Light that he would soon be living among. How he loved those visits! His favorite part was being able to ride Pegasus, the horse, and fly unfettered through the air. Free of pain. Free of fear. After a while, Gordy would bring the imagery to an end, and Andraez would drift gently back into his little body.

This time, there would be no return.

Words catching in his dry throat, Gordy managed to speak softly to his son, "Hey, you know what, honey? You like it when you're over there. You know… you don't have to come back this time if you don't want to. You could have Pegasus come pick you up right now, and you can fly with him and be free, just be free of this body. We'll catch up with you later. We'll be seeing you again."

Trembling, Joey sat on the side of the bed, unable to face her little boy in his final seconds, choking back her emotions while silently embracing him with the expansiveness of a mother's love. Consumed in a deep well of grief, she finally sank to the floor sobbing. The high-pitched buzz that had begun in her head the day she had first learned of Andraez's diagnosis months before screeched even louder now in an attempt to obliterate her pain. *Make it all go away! Oh God, bring my baby back!*

Since pushing off his mask, Andraez seemed comfortable. No more struggle. He rested peacefully. Final words whispered from his soon-to-be silenced lips were "When the wind chimes chime." Somehow Gordy understood … wind chimes. Hearing wind chimes would be a sign that Andraez was ever near, free like the wind yet still around. You can't see him, but you can feel him.

If you can feel. If you can feel *anything*. Learning to feel again would take time. It might take forever. Yet even on this day of their deepest heartbreak, they knew they had at least protected their child from a fate much worse.

Seven o'clock in the morning. His last breath. Seven o'clock on the seventh floor of the hospital on the seventh day since checking into the intensive care unit. Andraez was seven years old. His name was spelled with seven letters.

Seven. Rhymes with heaven.

The sun was just beginning to rise as Joey and Gordy's son rose in freedom from his little cancer-wracked body. Sunrise brought with it memories, a memory of the day Andraez had announced to Gordy, "Dad, there's a song called 'Sunrise,' and you need to download it." Gordy wasn't familiar with the song but found one by that name on the Internet, a beautiful song by Tony O'Connor. "That's the one!" Andraez had exclaimed, and from then on, he listened to it several times a day, drifting into a magical secret world in his mind, a blissful world of serenity.

And so it seemed appropriate that it was at sunrise on March 31, 2003, that Andraez Diego Lee journeyed home.

*Seeing death as the end of life is like seeing
the horizon as the end of the ocean.*

—David Searls

Chapter Two

It was during a much-needed vacation in Puerto Vallarta, Mexico, that Andraez had been conceived. Gordy and Joey had a use-it-or-lose-it time-share accommodation awaiting them there, so they invited friends to join them at the luxurious two-story beachfront condominium. Glorious days in the sun, filled with good food, good friends, and fiestas. They hired a local cook to come in and prepare wonderful, delicious meals for them. Days were filled with horseback rides through the jungle and refreshing dives into the warm tropical waters. Evenings were spent dancing under the dazzling canopy of stars and enjoying an array of musical events—all the activities that make those once-in-a-lifetime memories.

One anticipated vacation delight was the exotic local beverage called a "cocoloco." Almost as much fun as drinking it was watching the theatrical extravaganza of its creation as the bartender would shimmy up the tree, whack coconuts to the ground, then flamboyantly machete the tops off the fruit, leaving all the natural juices inside and adding four kinds of rum. Garnished with fresh flowers, tropical greenery, and a long straw, it was worth every mouth-watering second of the wait.

Before the vacation, Joey and Gordy had been trying unsuccessfully to conceive another child, but looking forward to those cocolocos, Joey decided to put that goal on hold for the time being. After all, if she were pregnant, cocolocos would be off-limits. However, the universe obviously had other plans, and their return home brought with it the most treasured little "souvenir" that would make itself known nine months later—Andraez.

Andraez's entrance into the world differed significantly from his brother Josh's birth four years earlier. When Joey had gone into labor with Josh, she was in the middle of a miniature golf game and didn't want to miss those last few holes! So she kept playing, stopping every now and then to double over with a contraction, then moving on to the next hole. Unbeknownst to them, several holes behind on the course was a doctor who discretely observed Joey's contractions. Finally, he came up to her and suggested she'd better get herself to the hospital. Never one to quit while she's ahead, she hurried through the last few holes, tallied her winning score, gloated over her stunning achievement on the course, turned in her club, then off they sped to the hospital!

Once settled into the maternity ward, they were faced with a long labor during which the room was filled with family members excitedly awaiting the arrival of the firstborn. As Gordy sang some spirited melodies and strummed on his guitar, he was soon accompanied by the doctor on guitar and several nurses joining in the singing. It was a jubilant time of waiting and watching (and for Joey, of course, pushing) until finally it became clear that a last-minute emergency Caesarian section was called for. The party was over, but a hearty, healthy baby boy soon came forth. They named him Joshua. On homecoming day, Josh was forced to go home wearing a pink cap as the hospital had run out of blue ones, but other than that minor early humiliation, life was good.

Four years later, Andraez's birth was just as joyous, yet a more private affair with only Gordy and Joey present. At first, Andraez was reluctant to leave his secure water world to emerge into the stark reality of the delivery room. After unsuccessfully trying to coax him out with a suctioning instrument which broke in the process, the doctor finally announced, "Well, it's time to get out the Kirby! We need the big one." And so he did. The lasting joke was that Andraez had to be sucked out of Mom's tummy with a Kirby vacuum!

The hospital stay was also prolonged as they waited for nature to call which was a requirement before Andraez could be released. Important to make sure everything was functioning properly. Success came after three days, and Gordy and Joey were finally able to take their new baby boy home to his anxiously awaiting big brother, Josh.

After a probation period of sleeping in a comfy bassinet in Mom and Dad's bedroom, Andraez finally graduated to the mint green nursery that was waiting for him. The walls were decorated with colorful Disney characters along with stuffed animals and bright mobiles that captured his attention. The little family of four was complete until about thirteen months later, when Zachary joined them. Zach's birth was a totally different experience from the other two. Joey had not even been sure she was in labor but went to the hospital just in case. One push, and five minutes later, there he was!

Being close in age, the three boys loved to play together and sleep together. Naptime always began with story time, and Mom would let the boys choose the books they wanted to hear. Their favorites were the Dr. Seuss series and Berenstain Bears. Sometimes if Joey was a little tired, she might try to skip parts of the story, but the boys knew the words verbatim and found wavering from the script quite unacceptable. So she dared not leave out a word. Later on, Josh would sometimes do the reading, and occasionally, Dad read to them, too, but most often, it was Mom's soothing voice that brought the stories to life.

By the time he was three, Andraez had decided that naptime was definitely not his cup of tea. Perhaps he sensed there was no time to waste sleeping. There was life to explore and precious little time to explore it. Part way through the storytelling, he would often try to slither off the bed unnoticed, off to greater adventures. His younger brother, Zach, would fall asleep right away, but Andraez would lie there for five minutes or so, then ever so imperceptibly begin to slowly slide off the edge of the bed. When Mom or Dad would ask him where he was going, he would respond, "Oh, I slept already." He just wasn't into the whole nap scene.

Since Andraez and Zach always slept together at night, pacifier-swapping became a nightly ritual. Often in the middle of their sleep, Andraez and Zach, just thirteen months apart, would reach over and take one another's pacifier. Sometimes one child would have two pacifiers in his mouth, or one in his mouth and one in his hand. Although each of the three boys had his own bed, there was comfort in numbers, and they somehow usually ended up all gravitating to one bed.

Sleepovers at their grandparents' house was another regular occurrence since Tata and Grammy lived just a few blocks away and spoiling the boys was, of course, their God-given grandparental right. Who could resist? Summer fun included bike riding, games, and splashing in the above-ground swimming pool in the backyard, but the biggest treat was the fully enclosed trampoline. It was safe since there was no way to fall out or catapult over the mesh wall, so it was their very favorite activity in the whole world, and they spent many hours seeing who could jump the highest.

Another summertime fun activity they loved was setting up barricades made of lawn chairs or whatever they could find. Josh and Andraez would then put Zach in a wagon or anything with wheels, plunk a helmet on his head, and ram him through the barricades. Oh, the joy of being the youngest one! They all thought this was absolutely the most hilarious entertainment of all … even Zach, the human ramming rod!

As with all siblings, the three boys had very different personalities, and those differences showed up in their morning wake-up rituals at Grammy's house. The boys would always wake up early, ready to jumpstart the day. Anxious for Tata to wake up, they each had their own way of making that happen. Josh's method was a big wham-bam jump on him and socking him kind of wake-up alarm! A definite jumpstart! Zach had a different modus operandi. He would just stand there and watch until his gaze became so palpable that Tata would feel its penetration and would finally open his eyes, much to Zach's satisfaction.

Andraez, on the other hand, was the mild one, the gentle one. He would very slowly pat his grandfather's face and speak to him softly, drawing him gradually out of the dream world. He seemed to have a sweet sensitivity far beyond his years.

Even though he was a shy child, Andraez was a chick magnet from day one! All the girls, especially older girls, wanted to be around him all the time. They doted on him, which of course, embarrassed him. His compelling eyes, his sensitive nature, his gentle ways—all could melt a girl's heart whether she was three or ninety-three.

Andraez loved dancing as well as all kinds of music. He watched Barney on TV religiously and always had a song playing in his head. When Gordy would take out his guitar, all three boys would squeal with delight and dance in endless circles, begging for special songs that they would sing along with. At the end of movies on TV, Andraez and Zach would always dance to the theme songs. Even in movie theaters, they would run down to the big screen and dance to the credits while audiences delighted at the boys' unabashed postfilm performances!

But Andraez's taste in music stretched beyond the typical children's fare. One day, he heard the song by James Brown called "I Feel Good" and immediately adopted it as his theme song. He would sing it over and over until the rest of the family couldn't stand it any longer. Then he'd sing it some more! Months later, after his cancer diagnosis, his grandmother, Polly, surprised the family with tickets to a James Brown concert in Reno. Andraez was so excited, yet at the same time, he was shy and wanted to make sure he would not be pointed out or called up onto the stage. Joey assured him he wouldn't be. The night of the concert was undoubtedly the thrill of his lifetime. He never sat down, he just listened in awe and danced to the rhythm of the music.

When he was about five years old, Gordy found Andraez listening to the music of the acclaimed pianist, Yanni. His favorite Yanni piece was the beautiful instrumental called "Felitsa" which Yanni had written in honor of his own mother. Andraez would listen to it again and again and said it made him feel good.

Andraez loved to immerse himself in his school work, too. He averaged about a grade ahead of other children his age, and although he had some classes in a nearby charter school, he was primarily homeschooled by his mom. Joey would carefully prepare two weeks of curricula at a time, but Andraez wanted to get it all done in one day. He loved the art projects and playtime, too, but he was most passionate about the lessons and would often want to keep working until he nearly finished the whole two-week lesson plan. Not wanting him to burn himself out, Joey tried to help him pace himself. Yet there were times when she would find him hiding behind the door in his room doing homework. So she would gently take the work away from him and usher him outside for some fresh air and sunshine.

Despite his unusual love of music and homework, Andraez was still a typical little boy who loved the things that all children love—birthday parties, Christmas mornings, trick-or-treating, and pumpkin-carving. Even then, his maturity and sensitivity were evident. Unlike most kids who go ripping through their birthday presents full speed ahead, momentarily appraising each one before tossing it into a pile and plowing on to the next one, Andraez would delicately unwrap each gift, taking his time, presenting it to each person in the room before carefully setting it aside to open the next one. Each thing was special to him, and he had that attitude of gratitude that usually shows up much later in life.

He also developed quite a flair for aesthetic decor when his grandmother taught him how to set the table for special occasions, how to fold the napkins all fancy and stand them up at each place setting just like in first-class restaurants. He knew exactly where every fork was to be placed, every knife, every spoon, plates one inch from the table's edge, tablecloth hanging evenly, candles in the middle. He did it all and took such pride in his accomplishments!

Another shining moment came about on the sunny spring day that Gordy taught Andraez to ride a bike. Since Josh had received a new bike, his blue bike had been passed down to Andraez, complete with training wheels. Finding the extra wheels to be in his way, he asked his dad to take them off, so he could ride big-boy style. He quickly acquired the art of balance and rode around the yard a few times. Within an hour or so, he called out, "Dad, look at this!" Gordy looked around just in time to see his son standing on the seat, posterior in the air, hands gripping the handlebars, cruising down the street! A child's dream perhaps, but surely a parent's nightmare!

Like many kids, Andraez wanted to be like his dad. He had big dreams of what he wanted to be when he grew up. Although Gordy had a full-time job, he also loved to tinker with cars, fixing them up and selling them, and he eventually started his own car lot, calling it "Kids-n-Cars" after his two passions. Through Kids-n-Cars, he donated some of his proceeds to four children's charities: Big Brothers, Big Sisters, Firefighters Pacific Burn Institute, and a domestic violence center. Well, it was pretty cool in Andraez's estimation that his father's business helped so many children, and he was determined that one day, when he was grown up, he would become the owner of Kids-n-Cars and would continue in Dad's footsteps.

But his dream of helping children went far beyond that as he also wanted to become a master healer, healing people using the "Force." In his playtime, he would use his hands like a Star Wars Jedi, using the Force to heal kids all around the world. Although this was prominent in his mind even before his illness, it became especially important to him after he developed cancer. He felt it was his unique gift, a gift that he wanted to share with the world.

So young he was, yet so wise beyond his years. In fact, once when Gordy and Andraez were in a huge metaphysical bookstore, a woman spotted Andraez from across the room and came running up to ask if she could hug him. She stood behind him and hugged him closely for several moments with her eyes closed. After taking a couple deep breaths, she looked up with tears in her eyes and asked Gordy, "What's wrong with him?" This was shortly after he had been diagnosed with cancer, but there were no outward signs at that time. Gordy was amazed that she could have sensed there was anything wrong. The woman said, "Did you know your son is an Indigo?" Gordy had no idea what an "Indigo" was, and frankly, he was a bit insulted until she explained that Indigo children are very gifted, often very creative and sensitive beyond their years. That certainly seemed to fit Andraez to a tee.

Precious Family Memories

Asleep on Mom's comforting shoulder.

The Brothers Three: Josh, Andraez, Zach

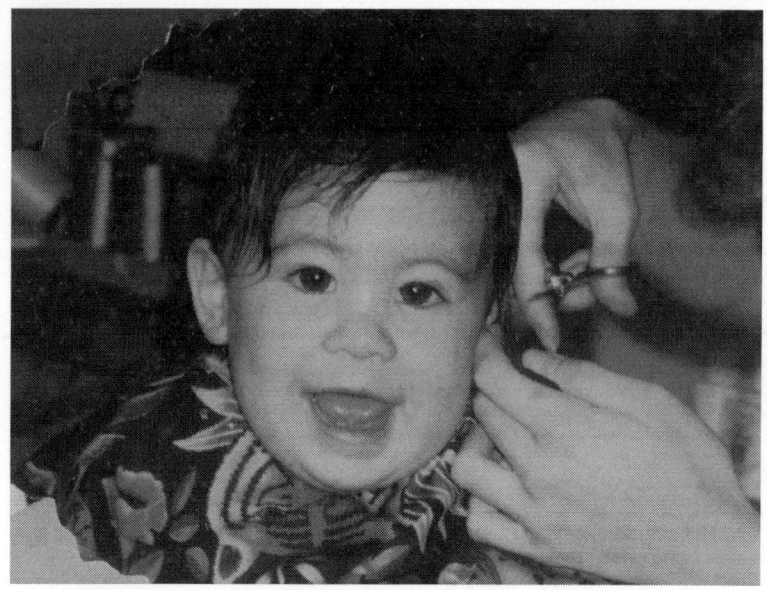

Andraez's first haircut

Let the pacifier swap begin!

Just us guys

The Lee family is complete. Joey holding Andraez;
Gordy holding Zach; Josh in front

Terror on wheels!

Trick or Treat! The boys' favorite holiday.

Grown men may learn from little children, for the hearts of little children are pure, and, therefore, the Great Spirit may show to them many things which older people miss.

—Black Elk, Native American Spiritual Leader

Chapter Three

There it sat, in the middle of a garage sale. Gordy had spotted the radio on a drive-by. Inspecting it closely, he noted the hand-scrawled price sticker—$50—a great deal! The lady who was selling it informed him that it had once been owned by Spanky of *The Little Rascals*. In fact, there was a picture of Spanky on the turn table. To some, it would be just a big clunky old piece of furniture, an old fashioned AM radio console with phonograph. But to Gordy, it was a treasure that reached back into his own childhood memories of *The Little Rascals*.

Lugging it home was no small task, nor was the decision about where to put it. Not too many places would it fit, but finally, after much debating, a space was selected in the dining room right next to the entrance to the family room. It was a busy corner, so everyone was cautioned about the new piece of furniture that sat where an empty space used to be.

It took some getting used to, especially if you were a little boy, especially if you were used to racing full speed ahead around the corner into the family room for favorite cartoons. It took only a few days for the awareness of this looming new obstruction to be forgotten, but only momentarily. Pain brought an instant recall of its presence as Andraez's left shoulder, which was about the same height as the console, crashed into the corner of it. He tried to shrug off the pain as he bravely fought back his tears. Thankfully, Mom was nearby and quick to the rescue. As a massage therapist, Joey knew the best thing to do was to ice it and have Andraez rest for a while.

After some tender loving care along with the ice, he cautiously resumed his play. The bruising would, of course, take time to heal, so Joey and Gordy kept a close watch on him. During the daytime, he didn't seem to be in too much discomfort; but at night, he would wake up crying, although the pain seemed to be as much in his elbow as in his shoulder. Finally, they decided to have his arm x-rayed to be sure his shoulder wasn't dislocated.

Since Joey worked for a chiropractic doctor, they took Andraez to the office where the doctor took a couple of x-rays. Looking at the x-rays, Joey noticed what looked like a puffy cloud that went down his arm. The doctor told her there was indeed a hairline fracture in his arm, but there was more than that. He advised her to take him to the emergency room as soon as possible because there was a "mass" in his arm.

A mass—Joey wasn't sure what that meant. Since a chiropractor cannot diagnose, he urged her to take Andraez to a medical doctor right away to have it checked. So with the x-rays from the chiropractor in hand, they headed for the emergency room where more x-rays were taken. Then came the long wait in the hospital waiting room where Andraez and his little brother Zach played quietly and did homework. Gordy was with them, too, but exhausted from a late night's work, he decided to go out to sit in the car and close his eyes for a bit until they were called into the doctor's office. A short while later, he saw Joey coming out to get him, murmuring something about cancer. When they came back in, an orderly rushed up to him and said, "We've got the x-rays back. It looks like it could be some kind of malignancy, some kind of cancer."

Cancer! It was the first indication Gordy had that his son might have cancer, and he heard it from an *orderly*, not even the doctor! Finally, a doctor called the whole family into an office and showed them perfunctorily the new set of x-rays, informing them that Andraez had a malignant cancer, a cancer that travels. Joey was in total shock, not only because of the horrible news, but also because of the nonchalant manner in which the doctor informed them in front of the children. No attempt was made to pull Joey and Gordy aside to give them the news, just a blunt diagnosis as though the boys were not even in the room.

The cancer itself had been there, lurking inside the child, eating its way through his bones. The jolt from hitting the stereo console had dislocated his shoulder, but the socket was so degenerated there was no point in trying to replace the bone. There was no socket left. The doctor informed them he would be continuing treatment the way it was.

More tests ensued in an attempt to figure out what kind of cancer it was. The doctor stated what he thought it looked like, but another appointment was needed to confirm his findings. Within a week, they had an appointment in a children's hospital where more thorough x-rays were taken. More waiting. More x-rays. Finally, the doctor called Gordy, Joey, and Andraez into his office and bluntly announced his findings, informing them of the seriousness of the situation. Exhibiting very little sensitivity toward parents or child, he simply stated that it was some kind of sarcoma. It was all the way from his shoulder to his elbow, and it was on the move. They would have to do a biopsy to determine the kind of sarcoma. He even went so far as to say he might have to amputate Andraez's arm. Gordy and Joey were horrified at the rude manner in which he delivered this heartbreaking news. A sickening feeling gripped them to their core. They just wanted to wrap their arms tightly around their little boy and protect him. How could a doctor so nonchalantly deliver a diagnosis that he must know would devastate them?

Yet there would be more tests, more poking, more prodding. Finally, they were sent to a university medical hospital because their medical insurance would only cover them at one of the two nearest hospitals even if there was a better-equipped one a little farther away! They had no choice. Nor did they have a choice as to what type of medical treatment their son would receive. As they were about to find out, it would be whatever the doctors dictated.

Although they had been told of the urgency of the situation, and that time was of the essence, yet their appointments seemed to be a pretty low priority at this hospital. At times, they would wait two or three hours for an x-ray because the scheduler had neglected to write the appointment into the book. Time after time, they would arrive for a scheduled appointment only to be turned away because someone had failed to record it on the schedule. Again and again, they would demand to speak to a supervisor only to be placated with excuses and promises. Exasperation and anger were added to the tremendous heartbreak the family was already enduring.

It was a long process of more and more x-rays, more and more blood tests, MRIs, and biopsies. Each time Gordy would question or object to the repetitive testing, he would be placated with, "We just need to be sure." After the biopsy where they removed a piece of bone, Andraez's arm swelled to twice its normal size. They were told the swelling would go down, but it didn't. Feeling a growing uneasiness with the way the case was being handled, Gordy began to carefully document all of the events including mishandled appointments, excessive x-rays, repetitive tests, and the attitudes of the medical personnel.

Finally, after a few weeks, they were introduced to a new doctor who would be taking over the case. He introduced himself and informed them that he was also a scientist. At first, they seemed to have a good rapport. He was more pleasant and relaxed than the previous doctors had been and certainly seemed more compassionate. They began to meet to discuss the severity of the issue without Andraez being present. No need to frighten him with all the scary details.

During their meetings, Joey and Gordy were disturbed to hear that this doctor was insistent on performing yet another major biopsy. They voiced their concern about so many tests. But not being dissuaded by their reluctance, the doctor said that, if necessary, he would bring the forms to their house for them to sign in order to *get* this biopsy. And so he did. As Gordy was instructed where to sign, he was dismayed at how extensively this biopsy was going to be used for research. No longer was it just about testing for what type of cancer Andraez had. No longer was it about helping Andraez. It was research! *Was this doctor/scientist going to be paid a lot of money for this research?* Gordy wondered. Is that what this was all about? Yet it became clear they had no choice but to sign.

It was the beginning of an uneasy feeling Gordy had about this doctor. One day, the doctor brought them in and told them that if the cancer was only in Andraez's arm, it wasn't so bad. There was an 80 percent survival rate, meaning an 80 percent chance that he could live another five years. If it had metastasized to any other bone, the survival rate drops to 40–50 percent . Yet it would be some time before Gordy would realize just how misleading such a prognosis could be.

"I've got some great news. His body is clear of cancer except in the shoulder. It has not metastasized." This reassurance came from the doctor following another MRI. With a wave of cautious relief, Gordy took the report home and began to read it, comparing it with another write-up by a different doctor whose specialization was interpreting MRIs. That doctor's findings were quite different. He had clearly written: "There are signs of this cancer on his ribs and in his lungs." High hopes came crashing down with a thud!

Since the first day the word "cancer" had been mentioned, Gordy had immediately put his business on hold and had begun to learn everything he could about childhood cancers, especially bone cancer. Although he was already relatively knowledgeable, he now spent every waking moment researching. He knew there were two kinds, and though he certainly wasn't a doctor, all of his extensive research pointed to osteosarcoma. He knew it in his heart even before the doctors confirmed it.

How on earth could this doctor have missed the report that clearly stated that the cancer was in Andraez's ribs and lungs? Did he even *read* the report? How could he raise their hopes like that?

Gordy was outraged! His own research, albeit layman's research, indicated his son had less than a 10 percent chance of survival. He had researched nearly three hundred other children in similar situations, and even if there was only a tiny spot of the cancer on the lungs, every one of them had succumbed to it. And it was a long, miserable ordeal leading to their death, primarily because of what was done to them. Cutting off legs, arms, parts of ribs, high doses of chemotherapy, vomiting, tube feeding, excruciatingly painful urination because of the chemicals. Yet every single one of them died anyway. Why put them through all that? Why? Where is the compassion in that? Where is the humaneness? Or is it for research purposes? Or fear of failure if a patient dies?

Gordy had joined an osteosarcoma forum and had been tracking parents of stricken children. Some of these families had substantial money and could afford Sloan Kettering, Stanford, and Mayo Clinic—all the best cancer hospitals in the world. Yet they, too, were losing their children despite the high level of expertise they encountered in those facilities. And the children had endured the exact same treatment that was now being planned for Andraez. Amputate his arm, part of his ribcage, part of his lungs, give him chemotherapy, radiation. And for what? So he could live a few weeks or months longer in total horror?

As Andraez's father, Gordy knew he must protect his little boy's dignity and his honor. There was no way he could hand him over and say, "Okay, here's my son. Go ahead and do what you want to do." That was out of the question. Surely, he told the doctor emphatically, there must be some kind of alternative!

Alternative … the forbidden A word.

His passion was met with an icy admonishment. "If you try anything alternative, we'll have Child Protective Services on your doorstep!" He was coldly informed that when a child is under sixteen years of age, there are no treatment choices in this state. Legally, the doctor's decision *is* the law. Gordy was advised of the possibility that he could actually be arrested if he did not go along with the doctor's plan and that Andraez could potentially be made a ward of the state.

With a sinking feeling of defeat, Gordy and Joey talked it over. Finally, they agreed to the proposed treatment only if they could get a second opinion. Managing to get Andraez's medical records and charts in their hands, they quickly found another hospital with hopes for a more open-minded view.

More x-rays, more poking, more prodding. There had been so many x-rays taken already! It's long been acknowledged that x-ray radiation drastically accelerates a cancer, so why keep zapping him with more? Why not study the x-rays that have already been taken? You could see the cancer very clearly. Cancer has already been confirmed. It just didn't seem logical to put him through more tests.

A team of doctors gathered for the final consultation with Gordy and Joey. The team included a surgeon, a pediatric oncologist, and one of the top reconstructive surgeons in the country. They laid the plan out on the table—in addition to chemo and radiation, they would amputate Andraez's arm starting at the shoulder, including parts of his ribs and lungs. Once again, Gordy pointed out his research and asked the doctors to give him some kind of assurance that his son had even a mere 10 percent chance of survival. They were evasive, unable to offer any hope for anticipated survival. In their stoic manner, they simply responded, "We can't."

Gordy asked the medical team what *they* would recommend as an alternative to their plan and was told he absolutely had to get his son started on some kind of radical chemical treatment right away, whether at their hospital or the original hospital. There were no other options that would be considered.

It was a painful time of introspection for both Joey and Gordy. So many mixed emotions. Andraez himself had fought all the testing, at times having to be strapped down just to get a blood sample. How could they keep putting him through this? And for what? Perhaps if the cancer were only in his arm they could bear to consider the extreme measures that were being pushed on them. But cancer having progressed to other bone tissue was, in their understanding, a death sentence. No one they had come across had ever survived that. What to do?

Within three or four days, the doctor called and informed Gordy that he had checked both hospitals and saw no indication that the treatment had been scheduled yet. He said, "Let me tell you something straight up, Mr. Lee. If you don't have an appointment for your son to put that catheter into his heart within twenty-four hours, I will turn you in to Child Protective Services myself."

Do we not all have a right, as we are dying, not only to have our bodies treated with respect, but also, and perhaps even more important, our spirits? Shouldn't one of the main rights of any civilized society, extended to everyone in that society, be the right to die surrounded by the best spiritual care?

—Sogyal Rinpoche,
From Tibetan Book of Living and Dying

Do unto others as you would have them do unto you.

Chapter Four

Through his lifelong interest in natural healing and his work as a hypnotherapist, Gordy had always gravitated toward natural methods as a first means of healing. He knew in his heart that the cure for cancer was not going to be found in the invasive treatments that were standard practice in the United States, and he was aware of alternative therapies used in other countries that had a high success rate. So when he first learned of Andraez's diagnosis, he immediately began to consider all options.

It so happened that a friend of theirs was a Chinese woman who had connections in China. She contacted a doctor there who reportedly had healed about two hundred "incurables," most of whom were Americans. He used integrative techniques including powerful herbs and Chi Gong. Immediately, he e-mailed back and advised Gordy to bring Andraez there as soon as possible, that he would treat him at no charge. It was worth a chance. They had to try.

With Andraez under the threat of becoming a ward of the state, they had to act fast. Passports were quickly and quietly acquired. It was right before Christmas, most of the presents were left behind under the tree. Since flights were expensive and their window of time was so narrow, they decided that Gordy and Andraez would make the trip alone. Joey would stay behind with Josh and Zach.

It was a tough decision to leave right before the holiday that Andraez loved so dearly and looked forward to all year. Yet Gordy recalled the stories he had read of parents who were in jail, whose children had been taken by the state and subjected to the prescribed horrors without even the comfort of having their parents with them. He could not allow Andraez the same fate. They had already been informed by their local doctor that he himself was taking the liberty of scheduling the appointment for Andraez and that if they did not show up for it, the boy would be taken from them.

And so it was just a few days before Christmas that their journey to China began. It was ten o'clock in the morning, and as the plane left the ground and was banking over the city, Gordy leaned over to look out the window. There, directly beneath them, was the very hospital they were supposed to be checking into at that very moment, ten o'clock! With relief, he snapped a photo. They had escaped the system … for now.

A twelve-hour flight on a 747 passenger jet is probably not especially appealing for most adults, but Andraez thought it was pretty awesome. There were movies on the big screen, food service, and the freedom to move around up and down the aisles as much as he wanted. The flight attendants were all in love with him. And of course, he was with his dad. All very cool indeed!

Finally, around ten o'clock at night, the jet landed. Wide-eyed stares greeted them as they stepped off the plane in Beijing. With his alabaster skin, black hair, and beautiful green eyes like his mom's, Andraez was somewhat of an anomaly. Everyone's head turned to stare and smile at the little boy from America.

They quickly spotted the Chinese doctor and his wife holding a sign with Andraez's name on it, and after an excited flurry of introductions, they all headed out into the seventeen-degree snowy night to find a taxi. A friend of the doctor had a vacant two-bedroom apartment on the thirteenth floor of a large apartment building that had been prepared for Gordy and Andraez to use as their home base during their stay. After the long hours in a crowded jet, what a welcome setting for the tired travelers! They were off to a good night's sleep.

The next morning, the doctor came back, this time accompanied by two of his friends as well as an interpreter. The two friends were very old Chi Gong masters from a six-thousand-year lineage of Chi Gong masters. It was very rare for them to make the journey to Beijing, but it was also quite rare for a child to come all the way from the United States, and they had humbly and freely offered their services in hopes that they could assist Andraez in his healing.

Unbeknownst to Gordy, using Chi Gong for healing purposes had recently become illegal in China. Following centuries of success in healing many incurable ailments, now the numerous huge Chi Gong centers had been shut down, and the Chi Gong masters were forbidden to practice it for healing purposes lest they be arrested. It could be used only for exercise, relaxation, or meditation. Gordy was told it had been an American-influenced decision based on trade between the two countries. Yet many, many stories circulated in the underground of healings of cancers and other fatal diseases

Through the interpreter, the masters conveyed their relief that he had not yet received chemotherapy treatments. In fact, they were shocked to hear that such radical choices as amputation and chemotherapy had even been considered by the western medical system since the cancer had already metastasized and was being carried throughout the body by the bloodstream. They felt it was an irresponsible and unconscionable decision.

Gathering around Andraez, the doctor and the other two masters stretched out their hands over his body and closed their eyes, sensing his energy. For a short time, they spoke back and forth among themselves in rapid Chinese. Then abruptly they bowed to Andraez, turned, and left.

Is that it? Gordy wondered. What did they say? Can they help him?

The interpreter came to Gordy and explained that the masters had identified Andraez as "one of the ancient ones," a very, very old soul. His purpose here was almost complete. He would not be staying in the physical body much longer. They said the cancer was the necessary vehicle for Andraez to leave his body, that there was nothing anyone could do to make him stay, neither their eastern nor our western medicine. No one could change the soul's journey, although they may be able to help him to be more comfortable in his remaining time.

It was a heart-wrenching jolt to hear it, yet Gordy had already sensed it was true. He was also told that he was the student, Andraez was his teacher. He must remember that. And he was advised to pay very close attention from this point on to everything and to learn because he would be continuing something important that Andraez was here to begin. Gordy's first reaction was "Wait a minute! I came all this way and spent all this money, and you're telling me my son is going to die?" Yet slowly, the reality of it began to sink in. There was nothing more to say.

It would be a time of deep soul-searching. What would be best for Andraez? Even though he knew in his heart that the Chi Gong masters were probably right—that his son's soul was ready to leave—time would be needed to absorb this grim news and to weigh their options. Returning home would mean reentering a stressful, chaotic situation at a time when it was so important that Andraez be in a calm, healing space. There was much criticism among family members about choices that were being made. There was also the threat of parental incarceration which would leave Andraez completely defenseless.

Believing in miracles and knowing that palliative care would at least be helpful in managing the tremendous pain of bone cancer, the Chinese doctor offered to do whatever he could to help. So the decision was made. They would stay for the time they had originally planned on and make the most of their time there. Over the next twenty-eight days, both Gordy and Andraez were taught Chi Gong techniques to help with energy flow. Reluctant to give up hope completely, the doctor created herbal concoctions for Andraez to drink, and even though these were horrible-tasting bitter brews, Andraez braved it. It was a huge achievement each time he reached the bottom of the glass, and they would all cheer!

Often, Gordy and Andraez would accompany the doctor to the local apothecary where hundreds of bins of fresh raw herbs, roots, grains, nuts, seeds, and other live substances lined the walls. There were varieties of living sea creatures and sea plants as well, all intended for medicinal purposes. The doctor would select the ingredients for his herbal recipe, and the pharmacist would carefully measure and weigh the exact amounts of each one, then grind them or emulsify them into a puree. Liquid substances would then be packaged in little glass jars, the dry ones wrapped in special cloth which would be carefully folded over four times and tied with ribbon.

It was an amazing process to watch, all items handled so mindfully. It was like going back in time, certainly different from our Western pharmacy shelves that are laden with thousands of prepackaged toxic chemical concoctions in pill forms that have most likely been sitting on the shelves for months!

Many of these plants were so nasty to the taste buds that it was hard not to gag. Yet hundreds of people had reported miraculous healings of incurable diseases including cancers. So even though there was little hope for Andraez's recovery, the doctor was not willing to give up. At the very least, these medicines would make his remaining time in his body easier for him.

Some people tend to fight their disease, but Andraez had embraced his cancer and had even named it. He called it Amocras. Perhaps naming it helped him to no longer fear it. Amocras was, of course, sarcoma spelled backward. It was much easier to reverse the word than the disease itself, yet befriending it seemed in order as it would be Amocras that would eventually lead his soul "home."

Though they longed to be with Joey and Josh and Zach, especially during this holiday season, it was a healing time for Andraez in many ways. He needed quiet time, away from the chaos at home, to discover himself, to feel who he was. He needed space to prepare his soul for the journey he would soon be taking. There was a quiet father–and–son bonding that could not have happened had they been at home. There were conversations that would have been forever lost had they not had this precious time together, just the two of them.

Gordy encouraged him to make a list of all the things he would like to do and to focus on them. Excitedly, Andraez came up with over one hundred things! Gordy had a cassette recorder with him, so he recorded all the things on the list, making them "I am" affirmations, and Andraez listened to them every day.

Despite the ongoing therapies, Andraez's arm continued to swell. Gordy's heart ached for his little boy whose time was running out. There was nothing more to do except to try to enjoy what time was left. After all, it was Christmas time, the first Christmas Andraez had ever been away from his mom and brothers and all the holiday traditions he loved so.

There's not a lot to do in Beijing in the wintertime, but they adapted to their new environment and managed to entertain themselves as best they could. In addition to daily Chi Gong and lots of walking, there were frequent invitations to restaurants and outings. Shortly after they had arrived in Beijing, they met a young Chinese woman named Katherine in the elevator of their apartment building. Andraez had smiled at her and greeted her in the few Chinese words he had learned. To his surprise, she responded in English! What a godsend to have someone they could communicate with. It would make their time there so much more pleasant.

Having the wide-open heart of a natural-born caregiver, Katherine took delight in reaching out to this child and his father who were strangers in a strange land. She understood the stress and loneliness they must be feeling and felt gratification in being able to help them feel more at home in their new environment. It was undoubtedly an enjoyable diversion for her, too, as she frequently offered to transport them around and show them the sights. Sometimes she would even take a day off work to drive them places that they would never have seen otherwise.

Gordy did everything he could to make their time in China as fun for Andraez as possible. There were fairs and ice skating and pottery making. And just like back home, there were indoor shopping malls, the nearest one being a fifteen-minute walk from their apartment. This quickly became a favorite hangout for them. Chinese shopping malls were quite different from malls in the United States. In a typical department store, all the counters were polished glass, and every single counter had one sales person. When entering the store, you could literally look down the perfectly straight row of counters and see ten to fifteen associates in their perfectly pressed blue uniforms, standing in rows at attention, waiting for a customer to approach their counter. Andraez found himself being somewhat of a celebrity as he walked through them. As soon as he would walk in the door, every person would see him, and one sales person would call to the next, like a domino effect, until all eyes in the store would be on the little fair-skinned, green-eyed boy from America! He felt like a superstar!

When they would call Joey and the boys back home, Andraez would squeal, "Mom, I'm famous here! Everybody knows who I am! They just stare at me, and I'm famous!" It was a big deal for this shy little boy. And back home, little brother Zach would ask Mom, "If he's famous, does that mean I'm famous, too, Mom?" Yes, Zach, you can be famous, too!

Food was another big deal for Andraez, and within walking distance of the apartment were McDonalds and Pizza Hut. One of Andraez's favorite treats in the whole world was a fish fillet sandwich. Gordy and Joey had been so careful with his diet and tried their best to keep his pH levels alkaline. No white bread, no fried foods, and certainly no sugar! Those all feed cancer. But how to you say "no" to your child when all he asks for is a fish sandwich? So every three or four days, they had lunch either at McDonalds or at the local Pizza Hut which served pizza with tentacles on it! Where else can you find a pizza with clams, fish, octopus, and squid? Pepperoni is obviously not a big seller in China!

Games were a good diversion for the father-and-son team, too. When they weren't in the mall, they spent time in their little apartment inventing a variety of games. A chair, a spoon, and a rubber band became a catapult for wadded up paper balls wrapped in tape. They would have competitions to see who could catapult the balls the farthest, sometimes reaching fifteen feet. Gordy had taken along a few of the Christmas presents from under the tree at home, and he bought a few more in Beijing, so the holiday could still be fun for Andraez. One favorite toy was a little power gun that shot a ring through the air. Other games were invented with the power gun, like seeing who could hit the most balloons that were placed around the room. All in all, it was the best Christmas it could be under the circumstances. Both longed to be home with Joey and Zach and Josh, but at least they had each other and created a deep father-and-son bonding.

As their time in China was nearing the end, one of Andraez's deepest desires was to see the Great Wall of China. He begged. He pleaded. It would have been a three-hour trip by bus, and Katherine had also offered to drive them there. Yet the doctor and the translator were adamant about the detrimental effect that it would have on Andraez's lungs. The air would be much colder there than it was in Beijing and very unhealthy for him. So the answer was no—a decision that Gordy would later regret. If he could go back in time, he would certainly have granted Andraez this final pleasure.

Christmas in Beijing with Dad. A father-and-son healing time in many ways.

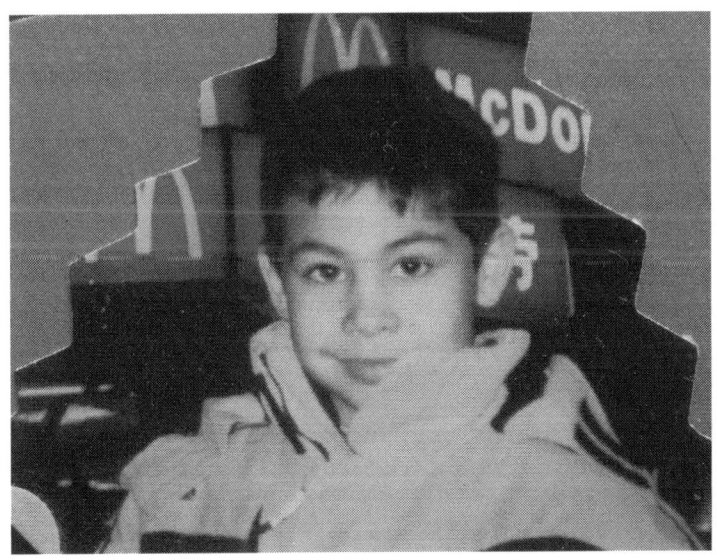

In front of a Beijing MacDonalds for Andraez's favorite treat, a fish fillet sandwich.

Chapter Five

A blustery mid–January came, and it was finally time to return home. Their friend, Katherine, had offered to drive them to the crowded airport. They were weighed down with all their belongings, including the extra Christmas gifts they had acquired and a treasured guitar that Katherine had shared with them and generously invited them to keep. So much to carry down the long corridors and stairwells of the airport! The terminal lacked the curbside checkers, the elevators, and escalators, and people movers that Americans have become reliant on, and although Gordy was carrying the bulk of their belongings, Andraez did have to carry a shoulder bag and small suitcase. It was a struggle for him, and Gordy's heart went out to the boy. Yet he couldn't possibly carry any more himself. After a transfer in Shanghai, they finally boarded the huge 747 that would carry them home. With a sigh of relief, they settled back into their seats to rest and watch the movies. For Gordy, it would be a time to reflect on their month in China and on his deep connection with Andraez. They had interacted at a deep level in ways that few parents have the opportunity to with their child. It had been a time of heart–opening, and in some ways, a time for closure.

It was Saturday when they landed back in the States to be met at the airport by Joey, Josh, and Zach along with grandparents and a few other relatives. As they all excitedly greeted Andraez with hugs, it soon became clear that their hopes for a miracle were dashed. They could see the boy had deteriorated. His shoulder and arm were clearly enlarged, and it was obvious there had not been the cure they had prayed for. In his phone calls from Beijing, Gordy had avoided telling the family what the Chi Gong masters had reported, that Andraez's journey was complete, that he would soon be leaving them. He had wanted to keep everyone in a positive state of mind. Yet now it was clear, and all they could do was love him. So they all went back to the grandparents' home and celebrated the Christmas that Andraez had missed.

The next afternoon, while Andraez was playing with the neighborhood children across the street, there was a knock on the door. Child Protective Services. Would they never give up? Perhaps they had been following flight itineraries, or perhaps they had been tipped off by one of the friends or family members who believed Gordy was wrong to resist the doctor's protocol. Some had even gone so far as to call him a murderer. They clung staunchly to the infallibility of the medical community. Yet the three hundred children that Gordy had researched—every one of whom had died a horrible, miserable death by allowing their doctor's intervention—had convinced Gordy and Joey that *that* would be inhumane. *That* would be murder. They must protect their child from becoming a statistic, not to mention a research subject.

As the CPS agent entered the living room, he noticed several guitars and other musical instruments around the room. Being a musician himself, this undoubtedly helped to break the ice, and after hearing the whole story of Andraez's plight, he seemed to be compassionate. Yet he assured them that the bottom line was if Child Protective Services wanted to, they absolutely could make not only Andraez but Josh and Zach as well wards of the state, the logic being that Gordy and Joey were irresponsible parents by not adhering to the doctor's orders. Deemed irresponsible parents would give the State the "right" to take all of their children away from them.

Gordy objected and stated that he and Joey were being *extremely* responsible and that CPS was making it tougher for them at a time when they should be helping them. How can they consider them to be irresponsible simply because they were seeking the most humane treatment for their son? The agent's terse retort was "Trust me. If we find a rat turd in your cupboard, we can deem you irresponsible parents."

He advised them they were absolutely required to set up an appointment with their doctor by the following Monday to be reactivated into the system, and they must report back to him when that appointment was made. It was impossible to resist this time, and they needed to buy time to figure out what to do next, so they reinitiated the process. This, of course, meant more appointments and many more x-rays which could exacerbate cancer cells.

Over and over, the x-ray technicians would have Andraez sit in front of a machine and x-ray his chest. Then, even though he had been perfectly still, they would say, "Okay, let's get that a little clearer," and they would zap him again. Parental protests ignored, there was nothing that Gordy and Joey could do at that point except try to put on a positive front, especially in front of Andraez. To argue with the authorities would only label them "uncooperative parents," and they feared where that diagnosis would lead.

Their previous experience at the appointment desk resumed as well with appointments being made but inexplicably dropped. This happened so often that Gordy began to document these miscommunications in his day planner. He would write down the appointment in his book in front of the scheduler, show it to her, and have her verify the date and time. Yet time and again, they would show up for the appointment and be told "Sorry. We don't seem to have you on the schedule." His demands to speak to a supervisor were always placated with put-offs and excuses.

Their final straw came one afternoon when they arrived for a two o'clock appointment and were told to take a seat in the waiting room. The chairs were hard and uncomfortable, and since there was no place for Andraez to lie down, he was forced to slump into one of the chairs and rest his head on the rigid armrest. Three o'clock came and went. Four o'clock came and went. Finally, at half past four, Gordy and Joey looked at each other disgusted and said almost in unison, "This is enough!" They were furious! No longer would they put their child's care into the hands of these people, no matter *how* much they were threatened. Their son's best interest was clearly not a priority here, and they were unwilling to play this ridiculous power game any longer. Having discovered the futility of trying to be heard, they were finished with this hospital! They were determined to find a better way.

The evidence Gordy was uncovering with his constant research continued to mount. Of hundreds of cases, he still could not find one instance where a child had survived this kind of cancer once it had metastasized. No matter how many body parts were cut away, no matter how many toxic chemicals were pumped into the body, death always came, and it was a death shrouded in horror.

Where to turn next? Through a medical doctor who had underground connections, they learned of a woman in another state who had been given a death sentence from her doctor and told chemotherapy was her only hope. Refusing the chemo and using her grandmother's herbal recipe instead, she completely cured her own terminal cancer and went on to help many other people—under the radar of course.

There was nothing to lose, so arrangements were quickly made for the whole family to travel there to see if she could help Andraez. Conveniently, they had relatives who lived not too far from the woman's town. They could stay with them. After settling in, a time was set up for Gordy, Joey, and Andraez to meet with her. However, at the meeting, it became clear that it was not a good match. There seemed to be some kind of resistance between her and Andraez. He didn't like her and did not want to go back. And after that initial meeting, she suddenly became unreachable. Perhaps she had succumbed to the fear of possibilities in trying to help this child. After all, what if Andraez died while taking her herbal concoction? What would be the legal ramifications for her? So she stopped returning phone calls, and it became one more dead end. What now?

While they were still staying there with relatives, pondering their next move, Gordy had a phone conversation with his sister. She had been an ICU nurse for twenty-four years, and in the beginning, she had been adamant that they allow the doctor to do whatever he wanted. Finally, Gordy presented her with all the research he had done and said, "Look, here's the research I've done. You have friends who are doctors, oncologists. Go talk to them. Do a little bit of research yourself, and then let me know what you find."

The very next day, she called him back, crying, apologizing. She had asked several doctor friends for their opinion. One of them, an oncologist, took her aside and said, "Don't use my name, and I didn't say this, but there's not a damn thing we can do for that boy. If it was my son, the best thing I could do for him would be to show him a really good time and give him palliative care."

In the meantime, Andraez's arm continued to swell. He could no longer ride his bike or his scooter because he couldn't hold onto the handle bars. His nerves were being affected by the cancer to the point where he couldn't use this thumbs to play his video games. All he could do was look outside and watch other children play. His time was clearly running out.

Continuing his desperate search for help, Gordy quickly discovered yet another medical doctor—this one all the way across the country—who was willing to take risks to help people. This doctor had nine medical degrees, and he happened to live in one of the four states where at least it was legal to consider complimentary medicine for children. They managed to scrape together enough money for Gordy and Andraez to make the trip while Joey and the other two children returned home.

On the wings of a prayer, father and son once again flew across diverse landscapes, finally landing at the nearest airport to the doctor. The weary duo made their way to their accommodation which was a special hotel where the doctor's patients and their families could stay for free. Gordy and Andraez gratefully settled in for a night's rest. The next day, they went for their appointment. After examining Andraez, the doctor turned to Gordy with a tear in his eye and gave the sad news. Had they come a month or so earlier, he said, perhaps he could have helped. But Andraez was already exhibiting blue veins spidering all over his body, a sign of the final stages of his disease. The doctor himself had lost a brother to cancer, and Andraez reminded him so much of his brother as a youngster.

Reluctant to give up completely, they decided to try just one week of the treatments which included nutritional and oxygen therapies, but nothing helped. On their last evening in the hotel room, they were resting on the bed with Andraez snuggled against his dad's chest. Together, they watched SpongeBob's Lost Episode. Andraez had been so looking forward to the program for a month, and having something—anything—to look forward to made it a top priority for Gordy as well. When it was over, Andraez reached for the remote and began channel surfing, suddenly stopping at a Tony Robbins infomercial for his "Get the Edge" program. Andraez was somehow mesmerized by the infomercial as he recognized Tony Robbins from the elevator scene in *Shallow Hal*, a movie that he had loved!

Watching intently, he asked Gordy what Tony Robbins did for a living, and Gordy explained that he was a motivational speaker, that he helps people with their lives and with their businesses. Suddenly, Andraez blurted out, "He's the one! You've got to write down his phone number. He's going to help you with the program." He was insistent that Gordy get paper and pencil and write down the toll-free phone number.

The program ... ah yes, it had been Gordy's brainchild and passion. He called it "The Secret to the Unlimited Child" and had begun to formulate it shortly after the birth of his first son, Josh. He had always yearned to help children experience life as it was meant to be—free and unlimited. He wanted to create something that would provide the tools to empower children, and he'd been busily gathering together all the information to launch the program when the news of Andraez's cancer put it abruptly on the back burner.

But Andraez's excitement about the program had never waned, and he wanted to be a part of it with his dad. Seeing Tony Robbins on the infomercial, Andraez had a sudden burst of insight that somehow there would be a connection with this man that would one day help his dad bring the program to life. He insisted that Gordy quickly write down the number.

Gordy had been leaning against the headboard doing healing energy work on Andraez who was resting against him, so rushing across the room for paper and pencil was not his priority of the moment. But Andraez was insistent that he write down the number, so he carefully extricated himself to search for a notepad in the hotel desk. How could he deny Andraez *any* wish at this point?

After hurriedly scribbling down the number, he returned to the healing, hoping he could relax Andraez and ease his pain. The warmth of Gordy's healing hands had always brought quick comfort to Andraez in the past. Even when he was younger and had had earaches, the energy would quickly relax him, and he would fall asleep again. As the pain in his arm had accelerated again, Gordy would put his hands on Andraez, and within moments, the pain would go away, and he would fall back asleep. By this point, however, his breathing had become so labored that he would constantly wake up during the night, struggling for breath even though he slept in a sitting position supported by many pillows. This evening, as they sat watching SpongeBob and infomercials, the energy no longer seemed to be able to ease his discomfort.

Worried, Gordy asked his son if he wanted to go to the hospital. He told him that they would be able to give him oxygen there and that it would make it much easier for him to breathe. When this had been suggested in the past, Andraez had always said no, but this time, he quickly responded with a yes. Gordy instantly began to fly around the hotel room, packing up their belongings as quickly as he could. The doctor had been kind enough to loan them a vehicle during their stay in case they needed to go to the hospital. It was a big Suburban, so high that Andraez couldn't climb into it, so Gordy carefully lifted him into the seat and fastened the seat belt. Off they sped to the nearby hospital.

As they rushed through the door of the emergency entrance, Andraez collapsed down onto one knee. Immediately, Gordy scooped him up and called out for help while several staff members came running, asking what was wrong. They got him admitted quickly and began, of course, more x-rays! Fluid had gathered all around his lungs, and they needed to take the pressure off. One of the doctors clumsily inserted a tube into Andraez's side to drain his lungs. It was horribly painful, and Andraez screamed at the top of his lungs. It was the first time throughout his whole ordeal that Gordy had heard his son scream—a sound that would be etched in his heart forever.

With the tube finally properly in place, the fluid instantly spewed out all over the wall, then began to fill a huge container. Relief came. When the draining was finished, they put Andraez on oxygen, and he was finally able to get some rest. As he slept, Gordy went out into the hallway and called Joey to fill her in on the evening's events. Needing desperately to be there with them, she made immediate arrangements to fly there the next morning.

Morning came. No amount of sunshine could brighten Joey's heart as she watched her frail little boy sleeping, exhausted from the night's ordeal. She and Gordy slipped outside to console each other and talk about what to do next. When they came back inside, the doctor came in and informed them that Andraez would not be able to leave the intensive care unit. He was too far gone. There was nothing left to do. They would not be able to take him home without a prearranged hospice situation as there would need to be oxygen and special round-the-clock care available. Here they were, two thousand miles away from home, facing the grim possibility that their son was going to die within hours or days. How would they even be able to transport his body back home? So many things that no one wants to face at a time like that but that have to be dealt with.

The doctor asked if they had ever had the Make-A-Wish Foundation come out. Of course, they hadn't! They had been in denial. Contacting Make-A-Wish would make Andraez's impending death seem too real. Yet they made the arrangements now, and someone from Make-A-Wish showed up the very next day laden with more presents than he could possibly have the energy to open. He managed to open only a few of them, keeping a teddy bear, a laptop computer, and a couple small items. While they appreciated the wonderful gesture, Gordy and Joey donated most of the gifts back to Make-A-Wish Foundation to be given to children who had time to still enjoy them.

One precious gift that Joey had brought with her from home was a binder that Andraez's friends and classmates had put together for him. It contained pictures and cards and many well-wishes, and it was his most treasured gift of all. He loved reading all the sentiments they had written to him.

Quick decisions had to be made about what to do next. They wanted so badly to take their little boy home but were told it would require a medical jet equipped with oxygen. Also, there had to be a doctor and a respiratory therapist on board. Oh, and the cost? Approximately $17,000! Their spirits sank even lower with this news. There simply was no way they could possibly afford that.

On Friday, a medical staff member came in and asked them if they would like to take their son home? Gordy responded tearfully that they had no way to do that. The person responded, "Well, here's what we're going to do. We have acquired a medical Learjet for you to take your son home. A doctor and a respiratory therapist have volunteered to make the flight there with you. You have half an hour to make it to the airport."

Gordy and Joey looked at each other incredulously. What a blessing! The ICU staff had created a miracle for them, and although it was hard to feel joy at a time like this, they deeply appreciated the generosity of these people. Finally, they could take their little boy home. In a quick frenzy of packing, they prepared to leave for the airport. They left many things behind as ambulances and Learjets are very small, most of the space being filled with medical equipment. As Andraez was transferred from the ambulance into the jet, he spied a TV monitor that was playing *Shrek*, another of his favorites. It would at least help to distract him and keep him relatively calm.

One doctor, one therapist, one patient, two pilots, two parents—off they flew chasing a fading sunset, soon cruising through a velvet night sky high over moon-drenched landscapes with intermittent glowing patches of twinkling city lights. Several times during the flight, Andraez's oxygen intake would drop, posing an increased threat of cardiac arrest. Each time, Gordy would rub Andraez's feet, and it would bring his levels back again.

Six hours later, they landed at an air force base that was the closest airstrip to their hospital. Having assumed that hospice would have their home all set up to receive them, they were surprised to be transported directly to the hospital instead of their home. Apparently, the decision had been made that hospital care was absolutely essential at this point, and indeed, it really was a godsend.

It was about midnight when they arrived at the hospital, drained from an emotionally stressful flight. As they entered the emergency room doors, Joey realized these were the very same doors they had entered the day they were first told Andraez had cancer. They had come full circle.

Andraez was quickly admitted to his awaiting room, and a place was prepared for Joey and Gordy to stay in his room to be near him. Over the next two days, several family members and friends came to see Andraez. One was Erica, a longtime friend of all three boys, almost like a sister to them. Hoping against hope, Gordy explained to Andraez that hospice had not been able to set everything up in their house on the weekend, but Monday was the day. On Monday, he could finally go home.

Monday morning came.

Andraez went home … to where wind chimes chime.

Andraez's ashes were solemnly scattered at his favorite
fishing hole where he caught his first fish.

A moment of contemplation. Andraez had three wishes:
I want to be a Master Healer.
I want to help save the world.
I want my book to help other kids with cancer.

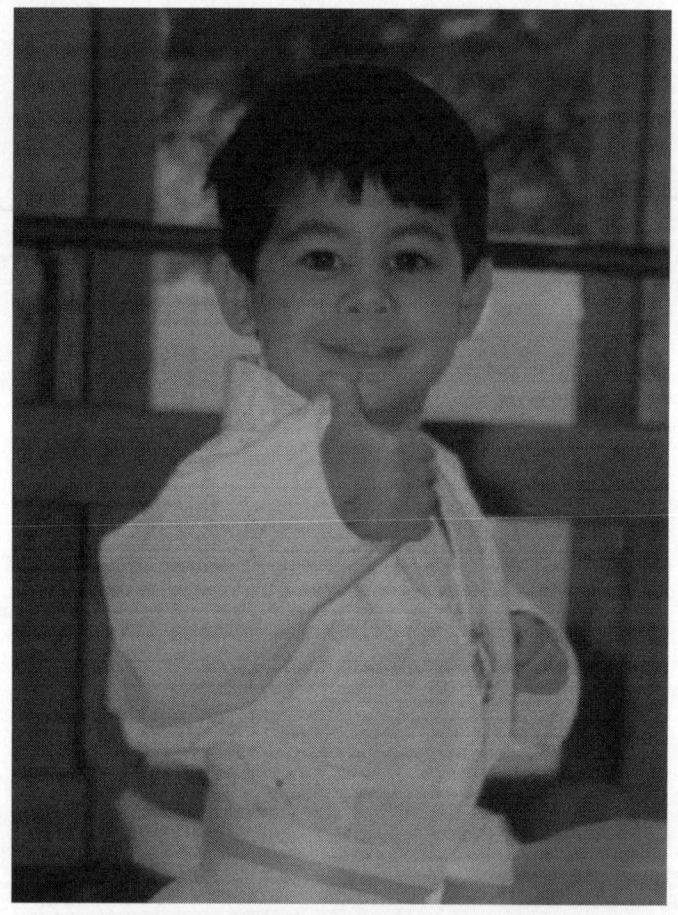
Thumbs up!
Andraez lived life big.
He departed this world as a champion.
His love for all carries on.

Chapter Six

The grief of losing a child is certainly one of life's darkest moments that most of us cannot even bear to think about. Indeed, death itself—whether it is of a child, a parent, a spouse, a sibling, or a dearly loved friend—is obviously a sad and heart-rending time for those left behind.

When I first learned of Andraez's story, I knew it was a story that needed to be told. His life and death must not have been in vain. I have shared his story with you—indeed, even with myself—that we may all get in touch with our own fears and feelings about death. Why? Because I believe that part of Andraez's life purpose—part of the "Soul Plan"—was to help us heal.

As we look at the *process* of death itself, the question is: How can we heal our experience of death? How can we come to terms with it, understand it, and embrace it? How can we release our deeply held fears about the inevitability of it? You see, most people on this planet have experienced death as something that has been devastating. It is this part of humanity's experience of death that can be healed.

In the second part of this book, we will have an opportunity—all of us—to delve into our own deeply held feelings and beliefs around these issues. For now, let's return to Andraez's story...

Thoughts that plagued Gordy and Joey were: How do you get up every morning and face each new day with such a huge gaping hole in your heart? How do you maintain your everyday functions—going to work, caring for family, caring for self—without giving in to the temptation to hide under the covers forever?

Added to the unremitting pain of losing their beloved child was the debilitating anxiety caused by ongoing threats that their remaining children might be taken from them, all because they wanted to protect the integrity of their dying son, to honor his life, to help him have a peaceful passing rather than a horrific, excruciating death.

Many are familiar with the research of Dr. Elisabeth Kübler-Ross who identified five stages of grief—denial, anger, bargaining, depression, acceptance. Gordy and Joey had certainly been through them all, many times. The denial: Maybe it was all a mistake, maybe we'll wake up and find it's all been a bad dream, maybe it will all go away. The anger: Why is this happening to us? Why to our sweet child? How could God be so cruel as to let this happen? The bargaining: Please, God, heal my child, and I'll do anything You want. The depression: There's nothing left to live for. And finally, of course, the acceptance, not because one wants to accept it, but because there's no choice.

Even in the shadow of Andraez's death, the drama would not be over for Gordy and Joey. For they had "bucked the system," and there's a toll to pay for those who have the audacity to hold on to their own values and not give in to the threats of the powerful.

Gordy owned a thriving car dealership called Kids-n-Cars through which he had been able to extend ongoing assistance to several children's charitable organizations. During the trip to China and for a month or so following his son's death, Gordy had asked a couple of acquaintances to handle the business in his absence. About a month after Andreaz's passing, Gordy returned to work only to discover much of his inventory, including tools and cars, had been stolen, and several payments had been pocketed as well, adding to his financial stress! In exasperation, he wondered what on earth he had missed about these people with whom he had entrusted his business. He had believed in their integrity and certainly in their compassion! How could they take advantage of someone at a time like this? But take advantage they did.

Hearing of his dilemma, a friend helped him to get his business back on its feet again by offering Gordy a line of credit which allowed him to replenish his stock. Things were eventually looking up for a short time until one day, he received a letter informing him that his business license was being revoked. The reason given was that he had not responded to a previous letter from the Department of Motor Vehicles about some paperwork that had been turned in a couple of weeks late. The original letter had been sent during the time he was in China, and since it was certified and required his signature, no one else could have signed for him. So unknown to Gordy, it had been returned to the DMV.

He explained the situation about his son's illness and death. Alas, the explanation fell on deaf ears. He had not responded to their letter, and they would, therefore, revoke his auto dealership license.

This didn't make sense. Through a concerned friend, he was introduced to a top DMV attorney, and they put through a request for arbitration. The request was denied. They would not even discuss it with him and kept bringing up the fact that he had failed to respond to their letter. Case closed. No more discussion.

This was unprecedented. No one had ever lost his license for a simple matter of paperwork being turned in a couple weeks late. Another attorney was called in to look at the situation. He, too, ran up against a brick wall. He said, in essence, "Gordy, I don't know who you pissed off, but this has nothing to do with cars and nothing to do with DMV. This is from higher up, way above the DMV. This is just a foible. Nobody should be burned for late paperwork. Maybe if it happens three times, perhaps a fine. But not a business license being revoked! This is incredulous! Something else is going on here."

It would not take long to discover the "something else." The dots were connected when they learned that the person in charge of the DMV had just transferred there from being in charge of none other than Child Protective Services. Gordy had raised their red flags. He hadn't given in to their threats. He hadn't adhered to the rules when he took Andraez out of the state.

Were they worried that he might make a public statement about the threats, the mistakes, and the way he and his family had been treated? Was this a threat to keep him quiet? Gordy wondered. Parents around the country would almost certainly have demanded, "What? They can make your child a ward of the state if he's under sixteen? What do you mean there is no medical choice?" But he had had no energy for that. His focus had been only on trying to save his son. He had simply disappeared from the grid, making every effort to find help for Andraez. Now it seemed there were those who felt he needed to be taught a lesson.

Gordy tried to save his business but to no avail. Some powers simply cannot be reckoned with. There was a brick wall, and he was once again up against it. He was forced to sell his remaining car inventory at wholesale, not even retail, and to vacate the property.

Financially as well as emotionally bankrupt, they were left with nothing but a taste of bitterness and a deep well of grief that threatened to swallow them up. Memories of happy times engulfed them, weighing them down, but they knew they had to pull themselves together and be strong. After all, they still had two precious sons who needed them, who needed life to feel safe and secure and normal again. And they *all* needed a fresh start ... away from this house of memories.

There was nothing left to do but move someplace far away from this most painful chapter of their lives. They finally put their house on the market, listing it at nine o'clock in the morning. They had a buyer by noon.

Time to move on. Let the healing begin.

Chapter Seven

Death—a love story minus the happily ever after. Where do you go from there? When your heart has been ripped wide open, when there's a gaping crevasse in the fabric of your being that nothing can fill. How do you even begin to mend it? Easier to remain numb, to hide in the busyness of life, to don the mask of strength even when you are crumbling inside.

Gordy and Joey had lost their child, never to hear his laughter ringing through the house again, never to watch his delight in catching a fish or throwing a ball, never to see him grow into a man. Zach and Josh had lost a brother, a playmate, a pal, a confidant, a best friend. Only memories left in their place.

There is an expectation that death will occur at the end of a long life well-lived when a person's journey is complete. We can accept the death of a grandparent or elderly person because we know they lived their lives fully. But the death of a child … what a seemingly cruel aberration of nature!

A mother's love is ignited the moment she intuits the tiny seed of life growing within her. Even as she softens into her nurturing maternal role, yet she can spring into warrior mode in an instant should anyone or anything threaten her child. Yet death had claimed Joey's child, and death is a force that cannot be reckoned with.

For Joey, sleep became her refuge, a place to pretend it had all been a horrible dream and that she would soon wake up to the sound of Andraez playing in the next room. Just as sleep was her doorway to denial, so, too, was staying busy. She never turned down a friend's invitation to do something, anything. It didn't matter what they wanted to do or whether she felt like it or not. She had to get out, away from the house, away from the memories. Keep the mind and body busy, go through the motions of normalcy.

She also found herself longing for the quiet comfort of nonverbal equine communication. As long as Joey could remember, she'd wanted a horse. Gordy had met a neighbor who owned a nearby ranch and several horses. One day, shortly after Andraez's passing, a new horse arrived at the ranch. It seemed a perfect time for a new addition to the family, so Gordy bought it for her. They named the horse Major, and he quickly began to pave Joey's healing path. Whether she was riding him or just brushing and grooming him, the bond between them began to melt the icy crust of protection that had formed around her fragile heart. She could begin to feel again.

During the time that Gordy and Andraez had been in China, Joey had started a project of helping her mother paint the outside of her house. The work had been put on hold since then, but now, recognizing the potential therapeutic value of busy hands, her mom encouraged Joey to finish the job. She did it all by hand and found the movement of painting, along with time to think, to be a catalyst for moving the energy of grief through her. Life was finally becoming bearable once again.

Everyone's journey through grief is unique. For Gordy, it was an especially painful time. Having spent nearly every hour of every day for many months with Andraez, there was now only emptiness. He hated being awake. Being awake was the nightmare. Every now and then, it would literally feel like the oxygen would disappear out of the air, and he would stop breathing and have a panic attack. His best friend for a while became tequila. Only after numbing himself with two or three shots for breakfast could he function.

He tried to be normal but normal no longer existed. Everything felt upside down and inside out. Nothing looked the same as before. None of the flavors tasted the same, none of the colors looked the same, and the air was different, the sunrises and sunsets—all different. Nothing was the same. He would get in the car, a car he had owned for three years, and it didn't seem like the same car. The car seat that had once held a little boy was no longer there. Had he taken it out? He didn't remember, but he must have. Just an empty space in the car now, like the empty space in his heart.

Gradually, tequila gave way to more important diversions as Gordy began to plunge himself once again into the work he had begun years before. The project that he knew would now become not only his emotional outlet but also Andraez's lasting legacy. Remembering his son's excitement when he had formed a company called Life Mastery Unlimited reignited his own passion now. Through his company, he had begun to develop the "Secrets of the Unlimited Child: A Children's Life Empowerment Program." (See Addendum A for more information on this program.) His goal was to provide life-empowering tools to help promote a higher quality of life for children and their families.

Throughout his adult years, he had been pondering the meaning of life and immersing himself in the many self-help books and programs that were available to him, trying to discover his own personal sense of purpose. In this process, a single thought kept coming to him: Why did he have to search so hard and so long for these answers? Why was he not given the proper tools for living life when he was a child? Why not make these building blocks available throughout childhood starting at birth?

The inspiration for the program had come to him with the birth of his first child, Josh. The death of Andraez brought with it a resurgence of energy to jump full speed ahead and bring it to its culmination. As denial started to lose its potency, Gordy poured all of his time and energies into further developing the program. He filled his office with photos of Andraez and forced himself to talk about him, to think about him constantly, to face grief head on. All of this became the catalyst for moving through his grieving process.

Healing is a journey that can take a lifetime, yet patience, gentleness, and compassion with oneself tend to soften the edges of a grieving soul. As the months passed, there would still be times when Joey and Gordy would spontaneously set the table for five before remembering they were now a family of four. There were moments of forgetfulness as they found themselves on the verge of calling the neighbor to remind Andraez it was time to come home for dinner. But although life would never be quite the same, it does go on. Joy and sorrow mingle to bring a subtler kind of peace ... in time.

Excerpted from *The Prophet*

Joy and Sorrow

By Kahlil Gibran

When you are joyous, look deep into your heart and you shall find it is only that which has given you sorrow that is giving you joy.

When you are sorrowful look again in your heart, and you shall see that in truth you are weeping for that which has been your delight.

Chapter Eight

There comes a time in all struggles when one must let go. The fight has either been won or lost. There's nothing left to fight for, to fight against, or to fight about. It's over. The whys and what ifs have become a moot point.

Still, Gordy couldn't let go. Not yet. He had to somehow wrap his heart around it all, make some kind of sense of it. Clearly, he could no longer fight the system, and he could no longer save his boy. But he had to find out … he had to know. Why did Andraez get cancer in the first place? What could cause a healthy, vibrant little boy to have bone cancer? And what about Zach and Josh? What about Joey and himself? Were they *all* at risk from this demon that had gobbled up Andraez's arm?

As his insatiable quest shifted to a new direction, his research began to lead him to sickening red flags as he discovered data that indicated a potential link between osteosarcoma and fluoride in drinking water. An article leaped out at him from his computer.

Cancer Causes Control. 2006 May;17(4):421-8.
Age-specific fluoride exposure in drinking water and osteosarcoma (United States)
Bassin EB, Wypij D, Davis RB, Mittleman MA.

Department of Oral Health Policy and Epidemiology, Harvard School of Dental Medicine and Clinical Research Program, Children's Hospital, USA. elise_bassin@post.harvard.edu

Objective: We explored age-specific and gender-specific effects of fluoride level in drinking water and the incidence of osteosarcoma

Conclusions: Our exploratory analysis found an association between fluoride exposure in drinking water during childhood and the incidence of osteosarcoma among males but not consistently among females. Further research is required to confirm or refute this observation.

Although this did not pose conclusive proof of the link, the articles he read certainly did indicate that a link was "biologically plausible" since fluoride is shown to deposit cumulatively in the bones and that the incidence rate would be strongest between ages six and eight when children experience a growth spurt ... and particularly in males.

Nausea bubbled up in Gordy's throat. He knew that the public water in the community they had lived in was highly fluoridated, but how could he have known of the risk of drinking it? After all, fluoride is good for us, right? It prevents tooth decay, right? Or does it? This assumption turned out to be not only theoretical but highly controversial, and as he discovered, dentists in the United States have been reporting increased cases of fluorosis which weakens tooth enamel, oftentimes a problem noted more in areas where the water is fluoridated than in communities that do not fluoridate their water. Many other countries have actually banned water fluoridation, yet in the United States, this toxin is being forced on us whether we want it or not despite the growing evidence of its potential dangers to our health.

Gordy continued to search for something—anything—that would reassure him about the safety of fluoridated water. Maybe the reports he had read were just overreactions. Maybe they were written by extremists. Maybe the fluoride levels in water had later been determined to be completely safe. Yet he could find nothing to convince him.

He came across a study published in 2006 by the National Research Council of the National Academy of Sciences that indicated fluoride levels in drinking water were considered safe for *adults*. It also stated that—based on body weight and daily water intake—infants and children consume up to four times more water than the typical adult. The EPA-approved dosages for adults give no regard to infants or children or the sick or the elderly. It would be like giving a child the same dose of medication that would be prescribed for an adult! Even our toothpaste labels warn us not to ingest the toothpaste, yet how many children love the flavors of it and consider it almost as good as candy?

Other reports indicated thyroid concerns as well as effects on the brain stating that fluoride accumulates in the pineal gland. So many startling statements, yet had the public been told about them? Were people informed about the risks? Was it really only after a threatened lawsuit that the EPA quietly recommended slightly lowering the level of fluoride in our drinking water? Yet our water affects all of us, so it was not surprising that a bipartisan group of legislators in Tennessee, noting a growing number of constituent calls, called for "Fluoridegate" investigations that would look into questions about why the CDC and other groups have not been forthcoming about the health risks of fluoridation.

So the law says we have no choice about what is in our drinking water or what chemicals are in our food or what toxins saturate the air we breathe, and the law says we have no choice about how we care for our sick or dying child. *Why have we given our power away?* Gordy anguished. Why have we bought into a system that would deny parents the right to protect their child, first from health risks and ultimately from being able to die peacefully from those risks? Why have we allowed a broken system to rule our lives and make decisions for us against our own common sense? How can we protect ourselves and our children from those who have a vested interest? These questions haunted Gordy and Joey.

In fact, millions of people ask themselves similar questions every day as they watch their constitutional rights being nullified one by one. What if we had free access to the numerous "healing miracles" that have cured thousands of cases of cancer and other diseases? What if we were told the whole truth about the risks of fluoride as well as the array of other toxic chemicals that are put into our very life support systems—food, water, air—or the risks of invasive medical treatments, so we could make our own educated choices? How many children and adults might still be alive? How much suffering might have been avoided?

Joey's love of horses brought to mind a story that was featured in Daniel Haley's book, *Politics in Healing*. It was in 1840 on a horse farm in Illinois, that a stallion owned by John Hoxsey developed a cancerous growth on his leg. It was recommended that the horse be shot, yet John decided instead to put the horse out to pasture. The horse seemed to gravitate to one favorite corner of the pasture to graze, and soon, the tumor began to dry up and heal. Hoxsey's curious mind led him to study samples of the plants and herbs that the horse would graze on. He experimented for months, finally coming up with several formulations which he began to use with great success with other horses in the area. Thus began the Hoxsey formulas which, on his deathbed, he handed down orally to his son, Harry.

Although not a medical doctor himself, Harry Hoxsey continued to use the formulas on animals as well as humans with great success, turning no one away. Over the years, his treatments were tested by reputable doctors and proven to work. At one point, a group of doctors wanted him to turn over the formulas to them. Knowing that they would charge high prices and would turn away those who couldn't pay, Harry declined their request. This eventually brought him threats and slander, ridicule and persecution despite hundreds of testimonials about his successful treatment of pathologically proven cases of cancer, successes that have been hidden by our medically-censored press.

Over the decades, there have been numerous safe, effective, nontoxic therapies that have saved lives. More are being discovered and proven effective every day. Yet the laws limit our choices to treatments that have been "approved" by our American medical establishment. It decides what will be available to us and what will be deemed unlawful, and any doctors who attempt to venture outside the guidelines set down by the medical rulers meet with harsh discipline.

BECOMING AWARE

By now, dear reader, you have undoubtedly given some thought to what *you* would do if your child were to become seriously ill or perhaps facing death. Certainly, it can be hard to know exactly how one would react until he is actually in a particular situation. Yet wouldn't you want the right to have some say in what happens to your child? Wouldn't you expect to be given some choices? Wouldn't you want to be able to determine when enough is enough?

According to Dr. Gina Cushman, NMD, PhD, under current laws in her state, if parents do not agree to have their child receive chemotherapy, radiation and/or surgery treatment, the government has the right to remove the child from his home. How can you be aware of *your* state's laws regarding a child's health care and his right to die once reasonable therapies have been unsuccessful? You can call your local legislators and ask them what your state law is. If they have no answer, you can inquire with your state medical association or state medical board or department of health. It is imperative that you educate yourself if you are to be empowered.

The best way to change laws is to educate legislators. Grassroots efforts demanding our rights may be the best way to preserve constitutional freedom of choice for physicians as well as for patients. One leading advocacy group that is working to turn things around is the California Citizens for Health Freedom (CCHF) which concludes that California has one of the most oppressive and restrictive laws in the nation on scientific advancement for the treatment of cancer. It states that under the current law, it may be a criminal offense for physicians to offer any therapy beyond chemotherapy, radiation, and surgery. A physician can permanently lose his or her license to practice medicine, and if criminally convicted, will go to jail.

Early in the 2013-14 legislative term, a bill will be reintroduced by CCHF to change the law to make safe and effective integrative treatment of cancer legal in California. Physicians would be able to offer the treatments. There will be full disclosure, so patients will understand the treatment and be protected against fraud. Parents and care providers will have the right to select a treatment approach from a licensed medical professional. (Details of this bill can be found in Addendum B.)

Passage of bills in bellwether states such as California affects many other states. For additional information about CCHF, go to:

http://www.citizenshealth.org/

Part Two

To Die Without Fear

Introduction to Part Two

Congratulations! You have made it to Part Two of this book. I want to thank you for hanging in there, for reading to the end of the touching, challenging, and often frustrating story of a little boy's death. It's never easy to hear such a sad tale. It evokes feelings we often want to deny or avoid. Yet this is where healing begins—with our feelings.

I had indicated earlier that the second part of this book would provide us with a place to go with all of the feelings that were generated in the first part. The feelings that we all undoubtedly experienced after reading this story can now help us to move to new levels of awareness and an expansion of consciousness. That is what feelings are for—feelings are the language of the soul.

Please know that I didn't just put you through all this for nothing. I shared this poignant story in order to open something in you, in order to touch some deep part of you that yearns to move beyond your fear and trepidation of the death process. So allow your feelings to fuel your receptiveness and awareness of what you are going to read next because the chapters that follow are going to ask you to search your own inner truths in order to discover what may be some beliefs that no longer serve you.

I believe this was the purpose for everything Andraez went through. In fact, I believe he's sitting here right now, watching you read this and saying, "Yes, now my departure from your physical world makes sense!" You see, your soul knows quite well why you are reading this book, and in the end, it has very little to do with Andraez. It has to do with your own journey through and beyond this life.

So in the following chapters, I will share some of my own thoughts and ideas as well as a variety of stories of people who have had experiences that helped them to die without fear. At the end of each chapter, you will have the opportunity to explore your own process in this journey. You are encouraged to have a journal or notebook handy so you can delve into your own story and see what you wish to hold on to and what you may be ready to let go of.

Okay ... let's move on, shall we?

Birth and death are the same thing.

You are continually in the act of creation,
in life and in death.

There is no such thing as the end of evolution.

—Neale Donald Walsch,
Home with God in a Life That Never Ends

Chapter Nine

Have you ever thought about the similarities between birth and death? Some people have equated the birth canal with the tunnel that those who have had near-death experiences have traveled through to the other side. There's even a light at the end of the tunnel, perhaps not unlike the glaring light in a hospital delivery room. And most likely, you will be greeted by loved ones or at least friendly faces.

These are some of the things I ponder on my frequent sojourns into nature. Mountaintops and valley vistas always inspire me, so I go there often. Driving the narrow, winding unpaved back country roads to reach the highest accessible point never fails to clear my mind and nourish my soul. It was a crisp and windy October afternoon that found me hiking around a volcanic rock formation called Rabbit Ears near the top of Mount Ashland in the Siskiyou Mountains of southern Oregon. Finding momentary refuge from the biting wind, these rambling thoughts flowed through my mind and onto a crumpled piece of paper retrieved from the pocket of my jacket:

> *Birth … death … birth … death … sameness*
> *Ever changing energy, flowing to and fro*
> *One's life ends, a new life begins,*
> *new vistas, new challenges, new blessings*
> *Eternity*
> *Life ebbs, life flows, always in motion, ever moving, never ending*
> *Why do we fear the movement of life*
> *its magnificence, its power, its beauty, its transcendence?*
> *Why?*

We call death the absence of life, yet there is no such thing
Life is
We fear that which does not even exist!
Why?
Embrace life in all its forms
Flow with it through body and soul, through planet and plane,
through galaxy and universe, through heaven and earth
Music, reaching deep, wrenching free the ancient emotions,
feeding soul, opening hearts, mellowing hatreds, soothing mind,
lifting spirit, harmonizing vibration
Wind chimes,
music of the spheres... announce the entryway to freedom.

Ahhhh, the entryway to freedom. What an exhilarating thought! Did the sound of wind chimes lead Andraez into the entryway of freedom? It seems to me there is a fine line between life and death, and I am convinced that the moment we cross that fine line, we will realize the line does not exist and never did. Like the lines on a map that divide state from state, country from country, lines are simply boundaries that we have invented.

So perhaps we have invented death, too! Just as some people see a glass half empty and some see it half full, some would insist death is the end of life, that with our final exhale, we move into nonexistence. Others might declare death is the beginning of a new life, an afterlife, or a continuation of life in a new way. We may look at death as a natural rite of passage or as a dreaded nemesis.

Truth be told, all of these are simply ideas—theories—beliefs of others that we have accepted as truths. None of us really know what awaits us on the other side of death's door, although some seem to have had a pretty convincing glimpse of it. One thing we do know is that that door will one day swing open for each one of us. Will we walk through it with grace? Or will we be dragged through it kicking and screaming?

We also know not *when* that door will open for us. Some say it may open several times during our lifetime, and we will be at choice as to whether we are ready to take that final journey. Many of us undoubtedly believe, or want to believe, that the door will not open until we are old and spent and ready to go. But the bottom line is, we don't really know when our moment will come. It may follow a time of extended illness, or it may come suddenly without warning. We may be an infant or a centenarian.

This morning, I read of a high school senior named Reggie, straight-A student, star quarterback on his Texas high school football team, who threw a touchdown pass, then collapsed on the field and died. Did he wake up that morning and say, "Today I'm going to die right after I make a touchdown?" I doubt it. Perhaps he was aware at a soul level, but I can't imagine he knew at a conscious level that this would be his last day.

In her book, *Being with Dying*, Joan Halifax recalled a meditation retreat she attended at a quiet retreat center in Canada some years ago. The group of sixty participants had been sitting in silent meditation when finally, a soft bell summoned them from their silence. Slowly, they each began to stretch and stand up in preparation for their walking practice, all of them except one. A young man, appearing to be in his late thirties and healthy, remained in lotus position. After a moment, his body tilted to one side and slumped over—he had died on the spot. Surely, he did not attend the retreat with a conscious knowledge that he would die. Did he leave his body during the meditation and simply make a decision to not return to it? We will never know. Ahhh, but can you imagine a gentler, more peaceful way to leave the body?

Although we may not know when our final moment will come, I believe we *can* prepare for it. We *can* be ready for it. And perhaps that is the real purpose of this book—to help us prepare and be ready. Children often have less need than adults to prepare as they are not so far removed from the "other side." For most of us, though, the first step is to be willing to talk about it, to get in touch with our deepest feelings and emotions around the topic. It cannot remain a taboo subject. Denial does not make it all go away; it simply makes the journey more difficult to traverse.

So this section of the book will include some accounts of people who moved through and beyond their fears and who embraced their own final days on this Earth with peace and dignity. We will discover various viewpoints and attitudes from past and present times about death and dying. And who knows, perhaps we will begin to formulate a new way to take our final journey—our journey into the Light.

When planning a vacation trip, there is much preparation required so we can be ready for it. So too the journey beyond this physical life to whatever comes next can be prepared for. And it begins by knowing who you are and how you came to have the beliefs you have.

At the end of each chapter, there will be a few questions designed to assist you in discovering more about yourself and your views about life and about death. It is recommended that you have a journal dedicated to this exploration. Find a time when there will be no interruptions or distractions. You may want to create a special sacred place in your home, a quiet nook where you will not be disturbed, a place with uplifting energy, perhaps with candles or soft music or whatever relaxes you into a contemplative and introspective state. Focus on each question for as long as it is comfortable. You may want to choose only one question each time. Write down all thoughts, ideas, beliefs, and memories that come to you. Be in your heart as well as in your mind.

Eventually, after you have explored all aspects of yourself and have come to see the root of your fears and have been able to face them, perhaps even release them, you may find yourself wanting to share your discoveries with others. Perhaps a friend or loved one is willing to have a dialogue with you. Perhaps you will be the person who helps another through his or her fears. Or maybe you will feel drawn to join or start a group for discussing these issues.

Let's look at our first questions for contemplation. Take out your journal and let the journey begin...

Questions for Contemplation

Thinking back to your childhood, just the first decade or so of your life, what were you taught about death/dying? Was there open communication about it, or was it a hush-hush topic? How did you feel about what you were taught?

As a child, did you lose any close family members, friends, or beloved pets? How did you cope with your loss? Were you able to talk about it with anyone? Did you receive professional counseling to help you come to terms with your loss?

What emotions did you feel free to express? How did you express them?

What questions did you feel free to ask? Who did you ask?

What emotions or questions did you hold back? Why? How did that affect your healing process?

Chapter Ten

As we surely felt from reading Andraez's story, the death of a child can be an especially heartbreaking event. We just expect miracles to happen when it comes to children, right? I remember assuming there would be a miracle for a classmate of mine many years ago.

Jill was a slender little girl with long curly brown hair and big brown eyes. At least that's how I remember her. She was my friend and classmate in the earlier years of grade school. One day, during roll call, as we realized she was not there, the teacher tenderly explained to us that Jill would be gone for a while, that she had a disease called leukemia and needed to go somewhere to have her blood purified. We didn't really know what that meant except that she would be gone for what seemed to us a very long time.

Weeks passed, or perhaps it was months. Then suddenly, one day, she returned to school, but she looked so different. That slender little girl suddenly had a chubby round face and an even chubbier body. Despite our childlike curiosity, we tried not to stare or ask too many questions. But our momentary awkwardness quickly melted away as we got used to the "new Jill" and didn't notice the change in her as much. Nor did we notice that over time, she became more and more slender again.

For several months, she seemed to be okay—"in remission," they said. Then one day, she was gone again. This routine of receiving blood transfusions and bone marrow transplants repeated several times. Then one day, we were told that she had died. She had fought her disease so hard, yet her disease won the battle. It never occurred to us that she would die. Children aren't supposed to die, are they? How was it for her? I wondered. Had she been afraid? Was she in pain? Wasn't there anything that could have saved her?

As I entered my teen years, I began to sense there was more to life than my schools or my religion were teaching me. I didn't quite know what it was, but I knew there was a much bigger picture than we–live–and–we–die–end–of–story.

My own curiosity about death began to form when I was quite young. My parents never sheltered me from funerals and wakes. It seemed as if we attended somebody's wake at least once a year. I never understood why they called it a "wake." Maybe they were hoping the person in the coffin would suddenly wake up!

I remember sitting unnoticed in a corner of a dimly lit funeral parlor, my nose accosted by the thick scent of floral arrangements that filled every nook and cranny of the room, and thinking that dying must be the most exciting part of life. After all, I reasoned, unless we're an ax murderer, we go straight to heaven, right? I would listen to the hushed tones of mourners as they stood in clusters, shaking their heads and whispering, "Isn't it a shame?" Sometimes I would cautiously inch my way up to peer into the satin–cushioned coffin to glimpse the pallid, waxen face of someone I didn't recognize. They reminded me of the figures I had seen at a wax museum at Niagara Falls where my mom and dad and I had vacationed one summer.

Oftentimes, the person was someone I had never met, perhaps a casual friend or acquaintance of my folks. Other times, it was a relative, someone I had been close to—a grandparent who died of old age, an aunt who died of cancer, an uncle who took his own life, a cousin who was killed in Vietnam. Even then, although I felt sad that I would not be seeing them again, I had a sense that they weren't in that coffin at all, that they were somewhere up in the corner of the ceiling of that funeral parlor, reveling in their sudden freedom, scratching their heads, wondering what all the sobbing and fussing was about. Maybe they were hanging around just long enough to be privy to what people were saying about them. Sadly, we often wait until someone dies to say the things we should have said when they were living.

My Presbyterian upbringing had taught me that life goes on forever, so my childlike mind often wondered why we found it so difficult to accept when a person actually *went* on. After all, they still existed somewhere, didn't they?

Later in my teens, I remember being captivated by Thomas Sugrue's book, *There Is a River,* a biography of Edgar Cayce—who was known as the Sleeping Prophet—and it changed my understanding of life, or more accurately, it verified my deeper understanding of life. Edgar Cayce was an ordinary man, a husband and father, a gardener, a Sunday school teacher, and a devoutly religious Presbyterian who read the Bible once for every year of his life. In his early years, he discovered he had a photographic memory when one night, he fell asleep with his head resting on one of his schoolbooks and awoke the next morning able to recite verbatim any page in the text. The dream of every schoolchild, I suspect!

As an adult, he developed an uncanny ability to put himself into a deep state of meditation and suddenly be able to tap into information about people he had never met, describing their physical diseases as well as remedies that would heal them, using technical or medical terms that he had no previous knowledge of in his awakened state. His accuracy astounded those around him and thousands of people came to him for "readings." He was also able to make predictions with a high degree of accuracy. More than fourteen thousand of his readings are still on file and accessible to the public at the Association for Research and Enlightenment (A.R.E.) in Virginia Beach, Virginia, which was founded to study and showcase his remarkable works.

I was particularly inspired by Cayce's life because he was a Presbyterian (as I was at that time), yet he believed in not only an afterlife but also in reincarnation. He called death "the process of passing through God's other door." His philosophy intrigued me and started my lifelong inquiry about the meaning and continuity of life. I came to discover that the doctrine of reincarnation was believed to have been included in the original Christian teachings. The Essene community in which many believe the gentle Jesus may have been raised espoused a belief in reincarnation. It was in the sixth century when Roman Emperor Justinian instructed the ruling cardinals to draft a decree stating that anyone who believed in reincarnation was a heretic and would be put to death. Feeling threatened that he would lose control if the people knew the whole truth about life, he had the biblical texts revised to remove references to reincarnation.

An insatiable desire was sparked in me to expand beyond the limited teachings of my own religious background. When I was nineteen, I moved to Washington D.C., to accept a government job, and it was there that I became even more curious and enamored with religion. In fact, I became a "church-hopper." Most Sundays would find me at an early-morning charismatic service at a local community Bible church where they really knew how to belt out the gospel songs that I loved. Then I would drive into D.C., just in time to attend a late-morning Methodist service on Sixteenth Street where I loved hearing the choir. The rest of the day would usually be spent either at the Franciscan Monastery or the Shrine of Immaculate Conception. Just breathing in the incense and praying in the candlelit catacombs fed some part of my soul that hungered for a deeper experience of Spirit.

Many weekdays, I would attend a mass at St. Patrick's Church either early in the morning before going to work or on my lunch hour. I couldn't seem to get enough. I studied Catholicism privately with a priest at St. Patrick's for nearly a year, and then took a class in another Catholic church for several months. When I turned twenty-one, much to my family's dismay, I converted to Catholicism. I remember telling the priest that I believed in reincarnation and asked him if that would keep me from being a "good Catholic." Looking around to make sure no one was listening, he advised me that although he could not speak on behalf of the official church, many of his priest friends believed in it, too, and they did not feel it conflicted with Catholic teachings in any way.

So I developed my own form of spirituality, embracing the aspects of religion that felt right to me and leaving behind the dogmas and doctrines that felt incongruent with my own truth. It was also during those years that I began to explore beyond the boundaries of traditional religion to read books that could be called "new thought," even though they expressed the oldest thoughts on the planet. Perhaps it was the work of Ruth Montgomery that had the greatest impact on me during my twenties and thirties.

Ms. Montgomery was a past president of the prestigious National Press Club in Washington D.C. She began her career as a respected Washington reporter and correspondent covering events in the White House under several presidential administrations. After writing a book about Jeanne Dixon, the psychic who had warned President Kennedy not to go to Dallas on that fateful November day in 1963, Ruth Montgomery began to look more deeply into the paranormal and soon discovered her own psychic gifts and talent for automatic writing.

From that point on, despite ridicule and criticism from her peers, her writings were spiritual in nature. She was given a fascinating array of information from the spirit world that would change my life and undoubtedly the lives of her millions of readers around the world. Some of the material that came through her spoke of a time to come when there would be much travail and death on the planet.

Having devoured her books one by one, I felt inspired to write her a letter expressing my appreciation for her work. I told her I was not afraid of the difficult times to come and felt the foretold changes would be an exciting time to be alive on Planet Earth. I yearned to be a part of the upliftment of the human race that her guides told her would be the outcome.

One day, a small envelope containing a handwritten note scribbled on a half sheet of paper arrived in my mailbox. It was from Ruth Montgomery, personally responding to my letter. She confirmed that although she herself would no longer be alive as the new millennium dawned, that I would indeed be here, and that during the coming times of great change, my energy would be needed to help quell the fears of the dying. She told me I would be helping people to die without fear. To die without fear—it would become a phrase held in some secluded corner of my heart to be explored "someday."

For many years, I have found myself fascinated with the numerous accounts of near-death experiences. Although they do not prove that there is life after death, they seem to offer some evidence that our existence does indeed survive beyond this physical realm. The term "near-death experience" or NDE, was coined by Dr. Raymond Moody who researched hundreds of cases of people who were declared clinically dead and subsequently revived. Not only did they report that they had remained aware during the time they were "dead," there were also many commonalities to their experiences while out of their bodies. One of the most well-known cases that Dr. Moody encountered was Dannion Brinkley.

They met at one of Dr. Moody's lectures. At that time, Dannion was recovering from being struck by lightning. Having been declared clinically dead for twenty-eight minutes, he reported that while on a gurney in the hospital, he came back into his body from a life-altering experience in which he was met by thirteen angels who set him on a new course in life. This fascinating account can be read in his book *Saved by the Light* as well as a movie by the same title. He has since become deeply involved with the hospice movement, having personally logged over twenty-six thousand volunteer hours at hospice bedsides, and recruiting over six thousand hospice volunteers. He also founded the Twilight Brigade, an organization that works primarily with veterans and offers free end-of-life care to all who ask.

I recalled that in his books, Dannion reported hearing the sound of wind chimes as he entered the passageway that connects the physical world with the spiritual world which many people experience as a tunnel. I found it fascinating that Andraez's last words had been, "when the wind chimes chime." In a phone conversation, Dannion explained to me that in his experience, one hears musical vibrations as their frequency harmonizes with the higher frequencies in the process that we call "death." These sounds often are described as the sound of wind chimes or choirs of angels or harps or other celestial tones. It is his belief that Andraez was already entering the tunnel when he uttered those words and that he removed his own breathing apparatus because he knew that breath is the medium that was holding him in physicality.

Even though I believe death to be a beautiful transition to something greater, it's, of course, especially difficult to face the death of a young child. It may appear to us when a child's physical life ends after only hours, days, weeks, or perhaps seven years that his life purpose was cut short. Yet we can never assume that we know the purpose of another's life or death. Everyone's path and process is unique. Every life has purpose and meaning. Every person comes into life with a gift to bring to those whose life he touches. And just as life is never in vain, neither is death ever in vain.

I find deep comfort in the following message received by Neale Donald Walsch and put forth in his best-selling book, *Home with God in a Life That Never Ends*.

> When you understand the endless and miraculous interweavings of life, every death is transformed into an event of enormous celestial significance. The

deaths of grandmas lying in sickbeds for years and the deaths of children darting into unsuspecting traffic and the deaths of AIDS patients and the deaths of test pilots and the deaths of people who died in peace and who died in violence, heroic deaths and deaths that go unnoticed—all deaths are elevated to the level of extraordinary meaningfulness, for every life touches thousands ... all death returns each soul to the truth of itself, to the truth of life, to the truth of God ... I tell you, no death is wasted, and all death brings a message to those who leave the earth and to those who remain.

Enormous celestial significance ... yes! I thought about Andraez and the celebration that surely greeted him on the other side of the thin veil that seemingly separates us from a world beyond, just as his life continues to be celebrated here among those who love him. I wondered—could it be that part of his purpose was to call attention to a medical system that had lost touch with the natural rhythms of life and succumbed to fear tactics instead of true healing? Could it be that his life and death would one day inspire amended laws that would honor all aspects of life and that would help to lead humanity back to gentleness, to a deeper compassion?

Perhaps his soul was drawn to become part of his earthly family to assist his dad in the creation of *The Secret to the Unlimited Child* program that would help guide children of the future toward their unlimited potential. What would this world be like if all children were told from the moment they were born how magnificent they were, instead of "bad boy" or "bad girl"? What if they were filled with self-confidence as they began to explore their new world instead of "don't do that" and "stop it, you're going to get hurt"? What if they were constantly reinforced with the knowing that they could succeed at anything they set their minds to instead of "you can't" and "you'll never be able to"? What if they were told that, as human beings, we are all interconnected, that our lives are all intertwined with one another?

Would there be as many gangs? Would there be as many wars? Would there be as many zombielike humans walking around zoned out on drugs and anesthetized by alcohol? Would there be as many unwed mothers, unwanted babies, broken homes, homeless people, abused children, social injustices, and environmental disasters?

Gordy's passion had been ignited as he thought of the possibilities for his program. And although the project had been put on hold during the attempt to get help for Andraez, it was never far from Andraez's mind. Near the last week of his life, he had snuggled against his dad in the hotel after watching SpongeBob's Lost Episode. Channel surfing brought him to the infomercial with Tony Robbins, and he prophetically exclaimed that that was the man who would help Gordy get his program out to the world. He insisted that his dad write down the toll-free telephone number.

Gordy had forgotten this incident until about a month after his son's passing. Then one day, as he was having lunch with a friend in a sports bar, a familiar voice suddenly came from the TV screen in the corner of the room. Looking up, he saw the same Tony Robbins infomercial, and immediately, the memory of that night came flooding back into his mind—the night Andraez had been admitted to the intensive care unit. To please Andraez, Gordy had scrambled for a piece of paper and had written down the phone number, but he had not given the number a second thought since that night, nor had he been able to open Andraez's little suitcase. Hearing the infomercial once again, he knew it was time. He must face the unbearable.

As soon as he got home, he went to the closet and took out the suitcase. Taking a deep breath and bracing himself for the wave of emotion he knew would come, he opened it. Touching the clothes, picking up the little shoes, breathing in the scent of Andraez—all brought a tsunami of memories and tears that he had tried to bury. He allowed the warm, salty liquid to flow down his face and drip onto his shirt. No need to hold back now. Finally able to continue, Gordy shuffled through the suitcase and found the piece of paper with the toll-free number on it. He immediately called it, and the very next day, he was introduced to one of Tony Robbins's Master Elite Coaches. She extolled him for his courage to protect his child's dignity and right to a peaceful passing and said she was honored to coach him. His passion to return to his project was reignited.

We are shaping the human beings of the future right now. I am often reminded of the late Whitney Houston's song, "The Greatest Love of All," that begins with the words, "I believe that children are our future. Teach them well and let them lead the way. Show them all the beauty they possess inside. Give them a sense of pride." We must ensure that our future leaders have the sense of pride and the confidence and the compassion that will make our world a better place to live.

Indeed, Andraez did not die in vain. No one ever does. Whether a lifetime lasts one day or spans one hundred years, there is always a deeper meaning for everyone whose life is touched by that life that ends. In truth, death is the illusion. Life is eternal. Even as we leave our physical experience, Who We Are lives on.

Of course, if we believe ourselves to *be* our bodies, the idea that life is eternal does not make much sense. There is a natural survival instinct in humans. We want to live forever—*in* our bodies. But when we realize that we are spiritual beings, souls who are simply using these bodies as a means of transportation, a vehicle through which we can experience life in a third dimensional reality, we can then begin to see there is a higher purpose to the transition we call death. Part of that purpose is through the life we live, the choices we make, the actions we take. Another part of that purpose is experienced through the way we pass on to the next form of life. We can make that transition consciously, or we can make it unconsciously.

In her book, *Sacred Contracts*, Carolyn Myss asserts that before it incarnates, a soul has an actual plan, a sacred contract or agreement to have particular experiences for its own growth as well as for those who travel along life's path with it. She uses universal archetypes or ancient patterns that exist in human consciousness to help her readers understand and fulfill their contracts. These archetypes date back to the time of Plato. One archetype which we all experience is the Victim. When we have a disease, it would be easy to view ourselves as victims. Yet seeing the disease as part of a soul agreement can alter our entire experience of it. It should be noted that contracts do not negate freewill nor are they based upon a belief in either reincarnation or in a single lifetime that is followed by heaven or hell.

Without a doubt, the pending death of a loved one is heartbreaking. Grief may engulf us until it seems more than we can bear. Yet even through life's darkest moments, there is a light that cannot be extinguished.

Pam and Lind from Ohio knew this well. When their nine-year-old son, Bobby, was first diagnosed with a rare and fatal hereditary neurological disorder called dystonia, their dreams were shattered. How could this happen to their sweet little boy? Yet the strength of their faith bolstered them and brought them even closer as a family. Sadly, Bobby died in 1995. Two years later, while still deeply mourning their loss, his younger brother, Eric, died of the same disease. In 2001, Lind died unexpectedly from cardiac arrest, perhaps a result of a broken heart. In that same year, Pam herself was diagnosed with dystonia, and shortly thereafter, her father was diagnosed with it as well. Pam died in 2006, leaving behind only their precious adopted daughter, Betsy.

How can one family endure so much tragedy, we may wonder? Was this part of a soul contract? What good could possibly come from this? Yet throughout their ordeal, this extraordinary family found strength in each other and in their faith that life has a deeper purpose. They experienced and expressed their sadness together. They found joys and discoveries along the way as well. They leaned on each other, grieved together, and were able to overcome their anger and loss. They found the strength to keep moving on despite each new heartache. And even in the midst of their sorrow, they created a program called Bobby's Books which uses books to help children and adults deal with difficult issues. Their lasting legacy continues to help children in hospice support groups to explore their feelings. This family will continue to live on in the hearts of all who knew them. (For more information about their deeply moving story and about Bobby's Books, visit www.bobbysbooks.org.)

Questions for Contemplation

As you went through your teen and young adult years, did your perspectives on death change or expand? Did a particular religious or spiritual background influence your understanding of death and/ or an afterlife? In what way?

As a teenager or young adult, did you lose any close family members or friends? How did you cope with your loss? Did you receive professional counseling?

What other types of loss have you experienced? (e.g., divorce, breakup, relocation, loss of career, loss of health, etc.) How did they differ from a loss due to death? In what ways were they similar?

Have you ever had an extraordinary experience such as a near-death or out-of-body experience? Can you describe what that felt like and what, if any, meaning it held for you?

What are your beliefs about soul contracts? Have you had any events happen in your life that you felt might be part of a bigger plan?

Chapter Eleven

Fear—the building block of negativity, the driving force behind every issue we face on this planet. It invades our thoughts, rules our actions and our reactions and affects our choices, our decisions, our responses, and our every experience. Some say it is used to keep us under control of something, someone. We must begin to look more deeply at our fears. What are they really about? What are we so afraid of? And at what point do we stop allowing fear its power in our lives?

Pollsters tell us the number one fear is public speaking, followed closely by the fear of death. The age-old hackneyed joke is that people would rather die than get up in front of people and speak. Truth be told, however, the fear of death most likely *is* the number one fear because for most of us, it's venturing into unknown territory, or at least unremembered territory, and we humans are creatures of our comfort zones, aren't we?

Of course, not all fear is unwarranted. Intended to be a protective mechanism, fear certainly has its place. Hopefully, it keeps us from standing in the middle of a railroad track shouting, "Hey look, here comes a train!" or crawling into a pit of venomous snakes just to find out how many are in there!

But fear used as a control mechanism to limit the freewill of others is not appropriate. When I heard about the threats and demands and insensitivity of some of the medical staff toward Andraez and his family, it seemed to be fueled by an underlying fear. I wondered how we ever got to this point. How did we, as species, move so far away from trusting the innate intelligence of nature? When did we begin to think of death as a failure, as something we must try to outrun at all costs, as if we could?

It's natural, of course, to have anxiety as one first encounters the reality of a terminal diagnosis and pending death. We fear the pain and its management. We mourn the possible loss of our capacities and our dignity. We dread the impact all of this may have on our relationships. Oftentimes, these fears are what motivate us to demand heroic medical interventions, regardless of the diminished quality of life that may result. As expressed by philosopher Michel de Montaigne: "The man who fears suffering is already suffering from what he fears."

Yet life itself has shown us that the death of the physical body is inevitable and natural at this stage in the human evolutionary journey and that it can actually be a peaceful experience. Should our transition from this physical realm require the permission of the medical industry?

From the moment we are born, we begin to move forward through our life span toward our final moment. No one can say how long a lifetime "should" be. Yet oftentimes, our medical establishment looks at prolonging life as their success and the end of a life as their personal failure. It must, of course, be stressful for a doctor when a patient dies, especially a very young patient who has been under his or her trusted care. Yet that does not excuse the coldness of a medical system that denies the right of loving parents to protect the dignity of their child when hope for recovery is gone.

This is not to negate the viability of medical intervention when it is chosen and when there is a strong possibility for recovery. And perhaps some parents would choose amputations, chemotherapy, and radiation for their child in order to hold on for a few more precious weeks or months regardless of the quality of life. This is not to challenge that choice or to make it wrong. Nor is it to say the choices Gordy and Joey made were the only right ones. This is simply to encourage us to look more deeply into our motivations for such actions. Whose interest are we protecting? Is it for the child or for ourselves that we would go to extreme measures for borrowed time?

It is also not my intention to challenge the efficacy of Child Protection Laws for they are absolutely necessary. There are many caring people who are dedicated to the well-being of the innocent. Still, is it appropriate to label parents as "negligent" because of their determination to maintain the highest quality of life for their child and their willingness to allow nature to take its course when there is not even one percent chance their child will survive the invasive treatment?

Before I learned of Andraez's story, I knew very little about Child Protective Services (CPS), so I began doing some research and was shocked at the reported abuses of power I read about. Although the purpose of this book is not to delve into the topic of tactics reportedly used by CPS agents, I strongly encourage all people to do their research and become aware of what has been called by some "a broken system." There are numerous horror stories online of people falsely accused of child abuse, having their children taken from them for little more than an unsubstantiated, anonymous, fallacious report by a vengeful neighbor. One article that caught my attention was "How to Protect Yourself From CPS." How odd that we should need to protect ourselves from a protection agency!

A major whistle-blower was former Republican Senator from Georgia, Nancy Schaefer, who gained respect from both conservative and liberal family rights advocates for her courageous report on the corruption in CPS. In 2009, she gave a speech at the World Congress on Families in the Netherlands where she described how the US government was involved in human trafficking. There are articles and videos online featuring her speeches. I encourage people to watch them. Unfortunately, she and her husband were found mysteriously dead in March of 2010 amidst rumors that they were murdered for her work exposing this corruption and that it was made to look like a murder–suicide. Although that cannot be proven, neither can it be disproven.

Fear is a powerful motivator. We see it being used extensively in media advertising campaigns aimed at convincing people that their ailments can and should be relieved instantaneously by taking this or that drug. And most of the drugs have contraindications and side effects noted in the fine print that often create a need for yet another drug. Advertisers typically mask the side effects litany by showing happy, smiling people as the dire possibilities of taking that drug are being verbally spewed out with the cadence of an auctioneer. Who benefits from the marketing of all of these drugs? Seldom the patients. Could we benefit more by listening to the innate wisdom of our own bodies and the voice of reason rather than the hypnotic droning of TV commercials as they tell us what we need?

Many of us know people who take numerous medications yet have lost the vibrancy they once enjoyed. They often walk around in a zombielike haze, unable to recapture the joy in life. We may also know people whose response to disease has been to bring their body back into homeostasis by supporting its needs with better nutrition and improved lifestyle. Many have improved their health and cured their diseases naturally and go on to enjoy life. Yet these claims are frequently ridiculed or denied by the powerful industries and our choices are being systematically taken away from us because our health does not make money—our disease does. Nevertheless, loving parents should be able to explore these alternative possibilities before giving in to the pressure to subject their child to invasive treatments.

I am convinced that the vast majority of doctors are caring, compassionate people who become doctors in order to help their patients. Yet they receive very little, if any, training in medical schools about natural remedies or about dietary and lifestyle forms of healing. Too often they are taught to compartmentalize the body instead of seeing us as whole human organisms. They learn how to perform surgeries. And thanks to the pharmaceutical industry, they are indoctrinated with the so-called benefits of every drug imaginable. They may even receive monetary incentives for promoting a variety of drugs.

Yes, fear sells. Due to the compassion and determination of his mom and dad, Andraez was spared the horrors that would have befallen him had they succumbed to the fear tactics of the system. But the three hundred other children that Gordy had researched were not spared. They suffered at a time when they most needed to be comforted and prepared for their pending death.

I was intrigued to discover how attitudes toward death have changed over the centuries. It was not always seen as the dreaded nemesis. In his book, *Western Attitudes toward Death*, Philippe Aries gives a glimpse of what he calls a "tame death" as it was experienced in centuries past when a person knew innately of his impending death and prepared for it. He took to his bed and simply waited for it. There was a certain ritual, a protocol, presided over by the dying person himself. Death was a public ceremony and visitors were encouraged to gather around the dying one. People seldom died alone.

Children were always included in these deathbed rituals, and it was simplistic without a great show of theatrical emotions. As Alexander Solzhenitsyn wrote in *The Cancer Ward* [New York 1969, pages 96-97] regarding the attitude of death: "They didn't puff themselves up or fight against it and brag that they weren't going to die—they took death calmly. They didn't stall squaring things away, they prepared themselves quietly, and in good time, deciding who should have the mare, who the foal. And they departed easily as if they were just moving into a new house."

Death evoked no great fear or awe in those days which is why Aries termed it "tame death." Until the nineteenth century, says Aries, death was a solemn event but as banal as seasonal holidays. It was expected.

By the end of the eighteenth century, when hygiene was first understood, attitudes began to change. There was a new passion around death. It can even be seen in the art of that time which often shows people around the death bed overcome with emotion, crying, praying, and gesticulating. It was an era of which today's psychologist would call "hysterical mourning." This exaggerated mourning marked a point at which people accepted the death of another person with greater difficulty than in times past.

These days, the exaggerated mourning has given way to desensitization. There seems to be a dichotomy as, on one hand, we are reluctant to discuss death, especially as it relates to us or our loved ones. On the other hand, we have allowed violence to become our entertainment of choice as we flock to the theaters or the video stores to be fascinated by the most heinous crimes acted out on the big screen. We sit glued to the evening news mesmerized by the latest war, the latest murder, the latest rape, and the latest torture. Even our children are exposed to hours and hours of violence through our media. Death has become almost surreal… until it hits home.

Indeed, fear has captured our society in its lethal talons, and fear is self-perpetuating. It leaves us feeling alone and uneasy. The time is now, to acknowledge our fear—our fear of dying, our fear of living. To release it, to move beyond it, to remove our focus from that which is fearful… to that which is joyful.

Questions for Contemplation

What are your deepest fears in regard to dying?

What are your deepest fears in regard to living?

Do your choices of entertainment (books, TV shows, movies, etc.) revolve around negative or positive scenarios? In what ways do these things affect you?

From where do your fears originate? Have the things you fear changed over the years? In what ways?

Describe your worst-case scenario for your death? How does it make you feel?

The End of Fear

I heard a voice of silence resounding my ear
It told me of a time to come when there would be no fear
It said I had a part to play in that transcendent shift
I'd help them all to understand so the clench of fear could lift

The purpose of my life, it said, would be to lead the way
That all would know the glory of their "crossing-over" day
I'd help them all remember where they'd been before their birth
I'd help them all to see again their beauty and their worth

I'd tell them of the passageway that leads them into Light
I'd help them understand at last, there is no need for fright
I'd lead them to the pathway that ascends the mountainside
I'd teach them how to walk that path 'til they reach the other side

I'd point out all their loved ones, arms open to embrace
Awaiting their return at last to that Light-filled place
Yes, again, the voice of silence comes pulsing in my ear
It tells me that this is the time … we can let go of fear

Chapter Twelve

Falling in love is a wondrous experience, most would agree. As we move our focus away from fear, as we lose our fascination with the dramas and tragedies, the violence and mayhem, the wars and rumors of war that inundate our societies, we may actually find ourselves falling in love with life! I really mean it—we can fall in love with life!

Life is more than simply the antithesis of death. More than just the period of time that occurs between our birth and our physical death. Life is energy in motion. Our evolving sciences tell us that we are made of energy, that all things—animate or inanimate—are composed of particles of energy, and that energy cannot die and cannot be destroyed, it can only change form. The very life force that animates our bodies is pure energy, and it is constantly moving, vibrating, changing.

Life might be seen as a rainbow of energy pulsating through our bodies. Many healing traditions observe the energy system through a series of seven major centers located along the spine called chakras. Chakra comes from a Sanskrit word meaning wheel or circle, and each chakra is a spinning vortex of energy flowing through the body. Each chakra has a particular color and relates to a specific organ and a specific gland in the endocrine system. One way to gauge the health and vitality of the body is by observing the chakras. When the chakras are open and balanced, a person is in a state of homeostasis or wellness. When the flow of energy in a chakra is blocked or constricted, the area of the body associated with that chakra can be negatively affected and will ultimately develop disease if not brought into balance. Many people are able to sense the energy field of other people as well as plants and animals. Some people are visual and can see auras and perhaps the swirling vortices in their undulating colors. Others may sense the flow of energy with their hand.

I remember the first time I clearly saw a person's energy body or aura. I had been engaged to a man for a short time, and we were soon to be married. One day, through a miscommunication, he suddenly became enraged and was shouting at me. This was certainly a side of his personality I had never seen before, and in the days following his emotional explosion, I discovered many more dark things about him that I had not known about! It was clear to me that I did not want to share my life with someone who could be so easily provoked to potential violence, and I was so grateful to have found out in time! I decided to end the engagement. Of course, this man was extremely remorseful, but I was firm in my decision. Understanding that he needed to process our broken relationship, I agreed to meet with him one evening a week in a public place, so he could have whatever closure he needed.

One day, he called me to announce he had learned how to move his energy with his mind, and he wanted me to come to his place so he could show me. *Hmmmm… Was this some kind of lure?* I wondered. Or some new age equivalent of wanting to show me his "etchings" just to get me into his apartment! Should I go or not? Since I didn't really feel in danger in his presence, I decided to go.

It was early evening when I arrived at his place and cautiously entered his rather dimly lit living room. The degree of excitement he greeted me with convinced me he was sincere. He explained that he had learned to put himself into a light meditation and then project his aura out to varying distances from his body. Of course, I knew that this was possible, but I wondered about *his* motivation. Was this a parlor game for him, or did he consider it some kind of demonstration of spiritual mastery? It was hard to tell. Nevertheless,

I was willing to observe, so he sat me down on one side of the room, and he sat on a chair across from me about ten feet away. I sat quietly for a few moments as he closed his eyes, relaxed and took some deep breaths. After several minutes, I saw a bluish-white light begin to form around his body. It extended a few inches all around him. As I gazed at him, I saw the light move out to about three feet from him, then about six feet, then back to three feet, then a little further out. Eventually, he drew it back close to his body. A few moments later, he came out of his meditative state, and his aura was no longer visible to my eyes.

While I appreciated the opportunity to observe this manifestation of energy, I never really did know what motivated him. It was not long after that we had our final evening rendezvous at Denny's restaurant, so he could pour his heart out. We said our last goodbyes, and I never saw him or his aura again!

Although the energy of inanimate objects is not always visible to the naked eye, it's always there. The energy of plants can also often be clearly seen. One time, when I was traveling in the Pacific Northwest, I was driving around the Olympic mountain range when I spotted an intriguing, winding mountain trail. Deciding it was time for a stretch break, I pulled over and parked and began to hike up the rock-strewn path. Near the top was an inviting little clearing, so I sat down alongside the trail for a while to enjoy the breathtaking mountain vistas, a glorious sight that never fails to capture my heart.

The dry rocky terrain sloped down steeply from my perch, and I noticed several little clumps of colorful wild flowers here and there amidst the bare soil and broken bits of rock. Absentmindedly gazing at one flower clump, I began to see a shimmering effect around it. I squeezed my eyes shut tightly and blinked a few times to clear my vision, but when I looked again, the shimmering was still there. Then I began to look at all the other little clumps of flowers, and each of them was clearly emanating their energy as well. What a beautiful sight to see such vibrant life force streaming from flora among the seemingly lifeless soil!

Life force, or energy, can never die, it can only change location. When we "die," our energy body simply leaves the physical body behind and continues to live in a different way, unencumbered by the body. There are many people who have reported seeing people who are no longer in their physical bodies, in other words, visions of those on the other side of the veil.

My cousin, Ruth, is an amazing woman of compassion who has had many spiritual experiences throughout her life. One night, when she was around nine or ten years old, she was deep in a nighttime dream when she heard her name being called. Drowsily being pulled from her slumber, she opened her eyes to find a figure standing next to her bed. Oddly, she felt no fear, perhaps not even a curiosity, but she just looked at it with an inner knowing that it meant no harm. Gradually, the apparition faded, and she simply went back to sleep. Yet his message seeped deeply into her heart. She understood that it had been Jesus who had appeared to her, calling her to follow him, to study his teachings, to know that his presence would always be with her, blessing her, protecting her. And that she should be a witness to his love and spread that love to others. She felt as if she were being chosen for a role of helping other people to experience the love of God. Perhaps it was this experience that first set her feet firmly on her Christian path and sculpted the kind of life she would lead.

When Ruth was in her teens, her grandmother died. It was the night of Christmas Eve, and Ruth was already in bed. Her small bedroom was in the back part of the house, and her single bed was against the outside wall. Hearing the phone ring and her parents' conversation, she sensed what had happened. Something drew her to stand up and walk to the window. Looking up at the dark night sky, there she saw her grandmother walking away, toward the heavens. She was accompanied by two other beings. It was another sign that Ruth was to be a witness.

My cousin always knew what she wanted in life. Even from a young age, she knew she would get married one day, have children, and become a teacher. Those three things were her life's purpose, she was sure. And so it was. She married Jack. They had two sons, David and Don. And Ruth became a special education teacher until her retirement. They lived in a lovely home. Life was complete.

Over the years, Ruth has been a caregiver to many family members as they faced their final days. Death has never been a stranger to her. Her natural compassion, her gentle ways, her very presence have always brought balance and comfort to those around her. In 2005, her husband, Jack, was terminally ill and nearing the end. A special bed was brought into the house and placed in the family room as going up and down stairs was no longer possible. He wanted no visitors, only his wife and his sons. As his last day came, his final words were "Ruth, help me!" Then suddenly, he sat halfway up in his bed, looked intently up at the corner of the ceiling, lay back down, sighed once, and died. Grace led him home, into a land of peace.

Losing a child, no matter what his age, is surely life's deepest heartbreak. Don had had many challenges in his earlier years but had finally settled down, had a lovely wife and children, and had his own business. Life was looking up until he was diagnosed with terminal lung cancer at age forty-eight. It would be another test of Ruth's eternal strength in the face of death.

Sometimes it's hard to see the purpose of certain events until much later. One day, while Don was in the hospital, Ruth came out of a department store and was walking to her car when she was accosted in the parking lot. In the process of defending herself against a person who was trying to steal her purse (hey, you don't mess with Ruth!) she was shoved down to the pavement. Her injuries were severe enough that she had to spend time in the hospital recovering, the same hospital that her son was in. Now being attacked doesn't sound like a "blessing," but that event enabled her to be with her son almost 24/7 in the last two weeks of his life. She would wheel herself down from her room to his and sit with him, holding his hand. There was not much else she could do as he was losing his battle for life. But holding his hand was a comfort. Having his mom with him enabled him to feel safe as he left his life behind. And for Ruth, it was the deepest blessing of all. She had been the first one to hold his chubby little hand when he entered the world and the last one to hold his hand as he left this world.

The months went by. Healing, grieving. Gradually recovering her strength and her courage, Ruth decided to resume her walks in a nearby park that she had enjoyed before Don's illness and death. The memory of being accosted made the first few attempts less than pleasant. Even though there were always other people walking and lots of activity in the park, still, when she would sense someone walking behind her, she would freeze until they passed her. But she knew she was protected, and eventually, she was able to walk more confidently.

One day, as she was taking her usual walk, she noticed the park was strangely void of all the people she typically saw every day. It seemed quiet, not much activity. All of a sudden there was a woman directly in front of her! *Where had she come from?* Ruth wondered. Strange, she hadn't noticed her approaching until she was right there. The woman stopped her and told her there were three young men walking together toward Ruth. She felt they were stalking Ruth, so she suggested that they have a conversation so the men would just keep going. It seemed strange, but Ruth agreed, and they stood and chatted for several minutes. Oddly, Ruth felt very calm even as the three men got closer. She felt no fear or panic at all. The men were walking in complete silence, and as they reached the women, they suddenly all split off in different directions. It seemed clear they had meant harm but could not go through with their plan.

With the men out of sight, Ruth and the lady ended their chat and said goodbye. Still feeling remarkably calm and collected, Ruth resumed her walk back to her car. Turning around to wave, there was no sign of the woman. She was gone. She didn't actually see where she went; she just was no longer there. Seemed strange, even though she was familiar with the people who routinely walked in the park every day, she had never seen this woman before and has never seen her since. Eventually, Ruth recalled her dream of decades earlier when she received the message, "I will always protect you." She realized she had been sent an angel.

My maternal grandmother also experienced an apparition that brought her great comfort in her final days in a nursing home. Born in Sweden in 1889, Mormor (which means mother's mother in Swedish) was a hearty woman with a strong Nordic heart and a sharp mind that stayed with her all the way to the end. Her adult onset diabetes had claimed her left leg several years before, and one of my vivid childhood memories was of cringing as I'd watch her stick a needle into her thigh every day to inject insulin.

After the death of my grandfather, she had moved into a mobile home right next to my parents' home, so Mom was able to care for her. But after a couple of years, her declining health made it necessary to move her into a nursing facility where she could receive round-the-clock care. Life was clearly winding down, and she seemed to be merely biding her time before joining my grandfather and others who had preceded her in death.

One day, when my mother walked into the nursing home room for a visit, my grandmother greeted her with, "Guess who came to see me this morning?" Mom assumed it must have been the pastor of our church, but why would he have come so early in the morning? To her surprise, my grandmother described her visitor as a glowing man who suddenly appeared at the foot of her bed, beckoning her with his hand as if to say "follow me" then disappearing before her eyes. She had been wide awake and totally lucid, and she was convinced her visitor was Jesus. A feeling of acceptance and calmness seemed to envelop her in her remaining days before she slipped quietly into the peace of death

Sometimes those who have passed over ahead of us have an important message for us, and their presence can actually leave their imprint in the ethers even after the vision has disappeared. That was the case with my friend, Doris, a retired minister. Doris had been clairvoyant since her childhood. Her first experience occurred one day when she looked up in the sky and literally saw a vision of a flatbed truck with chickens in the back! It was being driven by her sister and brother-in-law. Although it didn't have any meaning to her, she told her mother about the vision. Her mother scoffed at the idea and told her it was the work of the devil to see visions. She told her not to pay any attention to it.

To their surprise, the next morning, her sister and brother-in-law indeed drove up in a truck loaded with chickens! Her mother was very afraid from that point on and told Doris to never talk about things like that. So she kept it to herself for a few years, but in her teens, the gift returned and has stayed with her throughout her life.

In the 1990s, after she had been widowed for a number of years, she and her daughter were sharing a house together in southern Oregon. Doris had become ill and finally went to a doctor who brushed it off as just a cold and advised her to go home and get some rest. That night, her daughter was awakened from her sleep by her deceased father as he literally appeared in front of her in her room. With her eyes open, she saw him manifest before her and heard him say, "Take care of your mother." Then he disappeared.

Stunned, she dashed into her mother's bedroom and said, "Mom, come look at my room, quick!" When they reached the bedroom, although the vision had subsided, the whole room was filled with beautiful little sparkles of energy that were clearly visible. Her daughter told Doris of the experience and her father's advice to take care of her.

The next morning found Doris even sicker. Heeding her father's advice to take care of her mother, her daughter convinced Doris to see a different doctor. As it turned out, she had pneumonia in both lungs and was immediately sent to the hospital for emergency care. She eventually recovered, yet she would have died of pneumonia had it not been for her late husband's appearance and words of advice.

These firsthand experiences as well as hundreds of similar ones recounted in numerous books have convinced me of the continuity of life, a knowing that can bring such comfort to those who are facing their final days. I also believe people have an innate sense when their own hour of death is approaching. My daughter has a friend named Julie whose father was dying at age seventy-four. His final days that summer of 2009 were spent in the hospital, and while visiting him one day, Julie noticed that he was preoccupied with running his forefinger down his arm over and over. Finally, she asked him what he was doing, to which he responded, "I have to separate the soul from the body."

Though not a religious man, he seemed to have a knowing that it was time for his soul to travel on without his body. A few days later, as Julie was sitting at his bedside, he pointed at the clock high up on the wall across from his bed and asked her to move the hands of the clock forward "so I can get to the end of this journey."

Some months after her father's passing, Julie came into her kitchen one morning and noticed the clock on her microwave was flashing the number 55. Assuming it was malfunctioning, she bought another clock that day and temporarily placed it on top of the microwave until she had a chance to have the microwave repaired. When the new clock also began to flash 55, her mother reminded her that her father had been known as Double Nickel on the CB radio for making people obey the 55 miles-per-hour speed limit. It's common in Polish families to go by nicknames, and he was called Double Nickel more often than his real name! Later, when she took her microwave in for repair, she was told that the panel was so burned up that it would probably have soon burned her house down! Like Doris's husband who advised her daughter of her mother's health emergency, it would seem that Julie's father was perhaps sending a warning of danger.

Many people have experienced a phenomenon known as "pennies from heaven" when a departed loved one seems to be putting pennies in their path as a way of communicating with them. Julie, too, feels her dad communicates with her regularly in a very cool way—by putting dimes in her path! Shortly following his death, Julie was on a camping trip, an activity she often enjoyed with her dad, when she found six dimes in places where you wouldn't expect to find change.

His courage and excitement about the next part of his journey had been challenged only by his concern for the well-being of those he was leaving behind. As Julie says, if he had realized how much he would still be able to communicate with those he loves, his passing would have been easier for him.

Over the years, I've come to see that it is actually possible for a person to experience peace and happiness as they prepare for their own death. I've seen it be a time of completion and emotional healing, a time of release and relief, a time of renewal, and a time of anticipation. Death does not require wailing and gnashing of teeth. If we are prepared for it, we may move gently into it. For many, death is seen as stepping into the beyond, into a world of light where we are free of all pain and sorrow, a world of bliss, of deep peace beyond our comprehension. For some, death is like being born again into a new world, being renewed in spirit, a new beginning.

It was in the late '90s, two years after her mastectomy, when a friend named Sunni discovered her cancer had returned and metastasized. Sunni's name truly mirrored her disposition which was always bright and cheerful and full of hope. Hope is an important part of a healing process, but healing doesn't always mean physical survival. Healing can be more about coming into an emotional and spiritual state of completion. That's the way it was for Sunni.

Sunni did a lot of work spiritually the last two months of her life to prepare for her death. She lived in a household of several women including her sister, Janet, and she had enjoyed attending Dances of Universal Peace every week in a local church. As her time drew near, Sunni and Janet spent much time reminiscing about their lives and planning the celebration of life that Sunni wanted after she was gone. It was important for her to share her life journey with those who would attend, so together, the two women designed an eight-page program that was filled with a collage of photos taken throughout Sunni's life along with her favorite poems, hymns, and sentiments and a synopsis of her life and her spiritual path which had taken her all over the world.

Her final days were spent peacefully in their shared home with her support team of women around her, surrounding her with love and encouragement. After her passing, Janet and the other women lovingly prepared Sunni's body and dressed her in the outfit she had chosen beforehand. They packed dry ice around her under her blanket and kept her in her bed for two days so that people could come and sit with her and say their personal goodbyes.

On the day of the celebration, at Sunni's request, a hole had been dug in their back yard in preparation for the planting of a peach tree. Her ashes were placed in a special cloth bag that she had received on Mount Sinai years before. It had the peace symbol on the side of it. After her grandchildren placed her ashes in the hole, the peach tree was gently placed on top, and we all were invited to come up and scoop dirt into the hole. This is a Jewish ritual that is usually performed at the cemetery after a coffin is lowered into the ground.

The celebration included many people sharing their memories of Sunni, and then we all gathered together in a huge circle in the yard and danced the Dances of Universal Peace. It was a joyous occasion mixed with nostalgia, and I remember thinking what a wonderful send-off this must be. Noticing one single bird that kept flying back and forth over the circle of dancers, I felt Sunni's presence in the winged one and sent her a silent bon voyage.

How sad that so often, our most loving words about a person are delivered after they have died. We say how much a person meant to us after they have passed rather than celebrate with them while they are still alive. David was one who chose to *attend* his own celebration of life.

David and Jo had met at Esalen Institute in Big Sur, California, where they were both doing a work study program. Esalen had a magical aura with its hot springs, cliffs, and canyons, drenched in salty sea breezes and vibrating with the rhythmic pounding of perpetual surf. One misty evening, while cleaning the hot tubs, Jo was feeling chilled to the bone. Noticing her shivering, David had crossed the room and put his strong arms around her to wrap her in his warmth. It was one of those electric moments that would live in their hearts forever, the moment a spark was ignited. Love bloomed—they eventually married and settled in Colorado.

David's lymphatic cancer was stage four by the time it was diagnosed in 1999, just a year after his open heart surgery. He and Jo had divorced, yet they still cared deeply for each other and saw each other frequently. Their relationship became richer after his diagnosis as he learned to open up and express his feelings. Disease has a way of opening a pathway to the heart. He had finally come to realize that love is not a feeling, not empty words. It was about who he was and how he showed his love to others.

His first round of chemotherapy was pretty easy for him, and he bolstered his healing with herbs and acupuncture along with various healers who came to offer energy work and prayer. He began eating a healthier diet including soups made with bok choy and other Chinese vegetables. His disease finally in remission, he continued with his regimen of acupuncture.

Spirituality formed an important part of David's life, too. His belief system was inclusive and constantly changing. He embraced many truths from many traditions and was especially attracted to Buddhism as well as *A Course in Miracles* and the Enneagram.

The relief of remission was interrupted by the return of his lymphoma. This time, the chemotherapy was more difficult. A couple of times, he seemed on the brink of death and his daughters rushed to his side. Yet he lived on. As his illness progressed, he was on many prayer lists. He belonged to a meditation group, *A Course in Miracles* group, the Center for Truth and Light, a nonviolent communication group, Dances of Universal Peace, and several other organizations. Each one had an extensive mailing list, so they sent out the prayer request to hundreds of people.

Finally, it became clear that he had to surrender to the fact that he was dying. He had three final wishes: he wanted to "die Jewishly," he wanted to die on a Jewish holy day, and he wanted to fly to California one more time, on his own, to see his two daughters and their families. Since he was not to be dissuaded from the latter, Jo took him the airport, watching sadly as he was transported to the gate in a wheelchair. Though weak and on morphine, somehow he survived the trip. When he returned home, he deteriorated quickly. It was time for Jo to figure out what it meant to "die Jewishly," so she arranged a meeting for David with a Rabbi and the hospice chaplain.

Humor had always been important to David, and he kept his sense of humor to the end, calling his relatives to say goodbye and joking with them on the phone. One particularly poignant moment for him was when he called his brother, and his brother said "I love you." For David, it was worth all his suffering just to hear those words.

Three weeks before he died, they decided to have a celebration of life while he was still alive. He invited nearly one hundred friends and relatives. As they gathered together, many shared their stories of times shared with David. Not long afterward, a few friends gathered in his living room to have a Rosh Hashanah service. Although he was weak and was on morphine, he smiled and managed to be present for the service. When the service was over, he lay down to rest, and that evening, his final wish came to pass. David died on a Jewish holy day. And one year after his death, Jo and a few others had an "unveiling" ceremony at his tombstone, which is a Jewish custom. Indeed, he died Jewishly.

The hospice volunteers said they had never seen such a rally of friends and family around a patient. David had been so present, not fighting it. He consciously let go at each step, dying gracefully.

Letting go—step by step. How blessed we are when we have the understanding and the opportunity to remain conscious throughout the process so that death may greet us gently, lovingly, peacefully.

Questions for Contemplation

Have you ever felt you were communicating on some level with someone who had died? Write about your experience and the emotions it brought up.

Have you ever had a vision or seen an energy imprint or felt energy? Can you describe it? How did you feel about it?

How do you want your life to be celebrated when you are gone? I would suggest you actually plan your own Celebration of Life as you would like it to be. This may be kept private or shared with a family member. Include your favorite songs, prayers, poems, or inspirational readings that you would like played, sung, or read. Select photographs that depict you at various ages and that highlight important events in your life. Perhaps write a brief "life story." This may be a project that unfolds over time, so take your time and be with this healing process.

Chapter Thirteen

We are living in times of turmoil as our beloved earth goes through her growing pains and birth contractions. A daily diet of bad news sprinkled generously with myriad forms of fear has led many people into a mire of hopelessness, depression, despondency. For them, peace may seem ever elusive, and life is no longer worth living. If we haven't walked in their moccasins, we can't really know the mind of another, what demons they may have wrestled in their past, or what fire-spewing dragons may be waiting to greet them around the next bend. Sometimes the best we can do is to be supportive and compassionate.

Any discussion about death usually leads to the controversial topic of suicide, whether assisted or self-inflicted. This always brings up an array of emotions, judgments, and beliefs. Here's the way I think about it:

If we understand that life itself is energy, that energy is not something that can cease to exist, that it can only change form and location, then we can view death as a transition from life being expressed through a physical body to life being expressed in another form. Contrary to what some have been taught, ceasing to reside in a physical body is not a "sin," and I am convinced that it is not an act that will toss one into a fiery hell for all of eternity. It is my personal opinion that this has been a false teaching based on fear and on the idea that an omnipotent God needs us to act in a certain way, or he will be mad at us and punish us. I hope we can move past the idea that God deals with things the way we humans do—with anger, revenge, retribution, punishment, jealousy, and so forth. What a small god that would be!

For me, suicide can be described as an action that shortens the time that life force remains expressive in one's physical body. There are many ways of shortening that time. Some people intentionally create an event whereby their life force leaves their body suddenly, through a conscious action, and we call it suicide. Others create a scenario whereby their life is shortened over a longer period of time through conscious actions such as smoking, eating a diet that causes disease, harboring hatreds and negative feelings that cause stress, drinking excess alcohol, taking drugs, taking risks, and so forth. This, too, is a way of shortening a life span.

We often tend to judge a person who shortens his or her life quickly, but if they do it slowly over a longer period of time, we dismiss it by saying, "It's his body. He can do whatever he wants with it."

I was sitting in class in eighth grade one day in 1960 when the teacher called me out of class to tell me that my uncle had died and that my mother was on her way to pick me up. Although I hadn't been especially close to Uncle John, he was, after all, family and the only nearby uncle I had. It was sad to know he would no longer be around for visits and family gatherings.

On the way home, Mom explained that he had taken his own life. Apparently, he had not been feeling well for some time but refused to see a doctor. Refusal to seek medical attention is often a form of denial and may be based on fear of what the doctor might find. Uncle John's lady friend had called my dad that very day to see if he would go over and talk to his brother and convince him to see a doctor. Dad arrived only moments after John had put a sawed-off shotgun in his mouth and pulled the trigger. The gruesome scene that greeted my father that fateful day was a horror that I'm sure haunted him for the rest of his life.

As devastating as a suicide is to the family left behind, we must feel compassion for the desperation that leads a victim to this final choice. People who elect to end their lives quickly do so because they are in unbearable pain, whether their pain is physical, emotional, mental, or spiritual. If their pain is emotional, it will go with them. They'll continue to be faced with it. Suicide is not an escape, nor is it a way out of emotional despair and anguish, nor will it dispel feelings of hopelessness. Whereas life itself offers infinite opportunities to work through these issues, suicide only delays and prolongs them.

A related topic of debate is what some called "assisted suicide," yet that term is an unfortunate misnomer. Marian Spadone, founder of A Fine Farewell, strongly prefers the terminology "aid in dying" for people facing terminal illness who wish to preserve their right to refuse invasive medical procedures which might prolong their suffering.

In times past, the word "suicide" has been associated with shame, and this is far removed from a desire to die in a gentle, dignified manner. As Barbara Coombs Lee, President of Compassion & Choices, says: "Suicide is the self-destructive impulse of a person who has every reason and ability to live. Aid in dying is the self-affirming decision of a person who cannot choose to live and can only choose the manner of an imminent death."

Until not that long ago, suicide was even said to be against the law. One of our more curious laws and a rather silly concept if you're trying to figure out how to put the "criminal" in jail! It was in 1980, five years after helping his wife end her unbearable suffering from inoperable bone cancer, that Derek Humphry founded the Hemlock Society which was committed to providing information regarding options for a dignified death with legalized assistance by a physician. Now known as Compassion & Choices, this organization is the largest, oldest, and most influential organization working to improve care and expand our choices and options at the end of life.

Humphry's work is largely responsible for Oregon's Death with

Dignity Act, enacted in 1997, which allows terminally ill Oregonians to end their lives through voluntary self-administration of lethal medications that are prescribed by a physician for that purpose.

Despite some misconceptions that have been flaunted by certain celebrities in order to sway people into believing their right to die with dignity is dangerous, nevertheless, there are very strict guidelines and criteria in place that must be adhered to in order to qualify to use the Death with Dignity Act. It allows only mentally competent, terminally ill patients who are suffering and who have less than six months to live, to receive a prescription for medication that will end their life in a dignified way.

One of the most well-known "right to die" cases that elicited debate across the country ended in 2005 with the death of Terri Schiavo, a brain-dead Florida woman whose husband and parents fought a legal battle for seven years—one in an effort to keep her alive artificially, the other in an effort to allow nature to take its course, so she could be free. In several public polls, it was clear that a majority of Americans strongly disapproved of federal intervention in the Schiavo case. A high percentage of those polled felt it was inappropriate for Congress to get involved in this way. Many felt that trying to keep her alive was more for political advantage rather than concern for her well-being or for any principles involved. This case did, however, start a dialogue among people who had not previously given much thought to such possibilities before the Schiavo case brought national awareness.

Many people assume that their wishes, as well as their advance directives, will be respected if ever they are unable to speak for themselves, but that may not be the case. In November 2009, the United States Council of Catholic Bishops issued a revised directive for Catholic health care which orders all Catholic health facilities to institute and maintain artificial feeding and hydration tubes in permanently unconscious patients, regardless of their advance directive instructions or family wishes. Some may assume this will not impact them if they are not Catholic; however, if you are in a Catholic institution, this directive applies whether you are Catholic or non-

Catholic. It is estimated that 30 percent of Americans receive health care in Catholic institutions, all of which must submit to the Ethical and Religious Directives for Catholic Health Care Services.

This "revised directive" is viewed by many as an audacious and arrogant act that takes away a patient's right to refuse life-prolonging care, a fundamental liberty that is guaranteed by the United States Constitution. Some feel the bishops have demonstrated a total lack of interest in patient choices that conflict with their own belief system and their directives. Some have posed the question, "Are these not the same ones who proclaim that all humans were granted 'freewill' by their Creator?"

At the 2009 Compassion & Choices Symposium, Barry Lynn, Executive Director of AU (Americans United for Separation of Church and State) said, "… it's important that Americans who believe that they have a right, using their own ethical guidelines and framework to make decisions, not allow the religious right or any other interest group to determine for them what their options, what their choices at the end of their life, will be."

Another speaker at the same symposium, Reverend Madison Shockley, Pastor of Pilgrim United Church of Christ in Carlsbad, California, had this to say: "A theology of compassion is one that posits that God and the attributes of God are essentially love and compassion for each of those God has brought into the world. And whether one withholds, or whether one withdraws, or whether one provides the means for an individual to choose to end their life at a time of unbearable pain and suffering … all of these are acts of love, acts of compassion."

I was blessed to know a brave and beautiful woman named Nancy who had struggled for several years to overcome her cancer. Finally, it became clear that there would be no return to health. Throughout her ordeal, Nancy had kept in touch with her many friends via e-mail to inform them of her health status and to request their prayers. As her final days were approaching and with the loving support of her family, she decided to utilize Oregon's Death with Dignity Act. As she neared her chosen time to leave this earth, she wrote the following beautiful e-mail to friends. I reprint it here with permission of her family.

My dearest, dearest friends,

Thank you so very much for all of your beautiful prayers, cards, emails, gifts, and flowers. They have brightened each and every day. I am writing to let you know I have decided to use Oregon's Death with Dignity. I will be leaving my body behind on the morning of Sunday, the 19th. I have been blessed with an overflow of love and divine spirit supporting this decision. My family has been beautiful in helping me and loving me. My journey has unfolded with so many amazing gifts of love and angelic friends. I hope you understand that because of my physical condition, I have been unable to reply and correspond as I would wish to. I am looking upon my new journey as a new birthday. Along with your prayers, I am asking that you blow bubbles and celebrate that I will be dancing once again. Please rejoice with my family. I plan to be moving into transition between 10:30 and 1:00 PM Pacific Time. I am so deeply honored and blessed to have you in my life.

Love and light, Nancy

Nancy's beautiful parting words provide great hope that it truly is possible for a person to not only accept but to embrace their end of life in a peaceful, life-affirming way. She absolutely *knew* that life would not be ending for her, and she celebrated! And she inspires all of us to celebrate life in all its forms.

Questions for Contemplation

What are your beliefs about suicide? How did you acquire your beliefs? Do you know anyone who committed suicide?

What are your views about "aid in dying" (also known as physician-assisted suicide)? Are there any circumstances under which you would choose it for yourself?

How would you react/respond if a loved one chose aid in dying? Would you support their decision?

Chapter Fourteen

"I'm ready to go. I'm not afraid to die. I've lived a full life, and I'm ready to move on!" These words had often been expressed by ninety-year-old Ginny, especially the last few weeks and days of her life. She was a one-of-a-kind woman who waltzed her way through life's ballroom, danced to the beat of her own drum, and lived life to the fullest!

She had been a member of our Toastmasters Club for twenty-five years and had rarely missed a meeting. When her beloved husband, David, was still alive, he had been a member, too, attending faithfully with her to the end of his time, even carting his own oxygen tank along with him to his last few meetings.

Ginny missed David terribly and so often reminisced of their life together, but missing him never kept her from relishing every day as if it was the greatest gift she'd ever been given. She was one of those people who could light up the room when she entered it, making her way around the room to give everyone a hug, always having a smile and an upbeat attitude about life. She could be feisty, too. If you asked her a question about politics or current events, look out! She minced no words and held back no opinion. We always knew exactly what Ginny thought!

Ginny was ninety years young, but she didn't believe in numbers, and ninety was, after all, just a number. She had always loved to dance and sing, so the number ninety wasn't going to stop her! In October of 2010, friends gathered to celebrate her ninetieth birthday with her. The party was held in a friend's lovely home in southern Oregon. Photo albums were displayed on a long table, so we could all catch a glimpse of her nine beautiful decades. A friend of hers had brought his banjo along to play some lively music, and Ginny became the main attraction as she danced along the poolside in the warm autumn sun. It would turn out to be her final party, and it was obvious how much she enjoyed each and every one who was there to honor her.

Just a few short weeks later, she had a health crisis and was given the choice of major heart surgery or of hospice care. Without the surgery, she was told she might have three months to live. Although surgery may have extended her life for a few more months or perhaps even years, there was no guarantee that the extra time would give her the quality of life that would make the pain of surgery and recovery worthwhile. For some, surgery may have been the best choice, but Ginny had no need to stay in a ninety-year-old body any longer. She yearned to be with David again, and she firmly believed that she would soon be dancing with him once again. She had absolutely no fear of dying, and she had no intention of hanging around another three months just waiting to die.

It was two days after Christmas, and I was scheduled to sit with Ginny from six to nine o'clock in the evening. When I called her at 5:30 to see if she wanted me to pick up anything for her from the store, a woman answered the phone and said Ginny had been having a difficult day with her breathing and that a hospice volunteer would be with her that evening. Although I offered to come anyway just to be with her, Ginny didn't want any visitors, so I said I'd stop by the next day instead. But at 9:30 that evening, Ginny's friend called to let me know she had passed away. When Ginny set her mind on something, there was no stopping her.

A week or so later, we gathered to remember all the things we loved about her and to celebrate her life. We watched slides and videos of her dancing and singing at her ninetieth birthday party. And we rejoiced in the knowing that she was dancing once again, this time, with David!

Perhaps this, then, is how we shall die—gently, free of fear, free of dread, with our hearts full of quiet anticipation.

As more and more "baby boomers" advance in age, hopefully, there will be a more rational, intelligent dialogue about end-of-life issues. Or perhaps "life-change" issues is a more appropriate term as we transition from life in physical form to life in nonphysical form.

There has been much technological progress over the past couple of decades, wonderful discoveries that bring ease and comfort to our daily endeavors. Yet we must use reason and common sense in light of the life-prolonging advances that can now keep people alive far beyond any quality of life and often beyond their own wishes. People must be empowered to make their own humane choices for themselves and for their children, rather than allowing the powers-that-be to dictate to them how and when they have permission to exit their bodies. It is time for us to regain control over our lives. And this can begin only when we are willing to have an open and honest dialogue.

No one wants to feel alone at the time of their deepest need. They yearn to talk and to be heard, to cry and to be consoled. They want choices and the freedom to explore all their options, not to be told someone else's "truth" is their only option. They want answers to the unanswerable, hope in their moments of hopelessness. They need spiritual care along with physical and emotional care.

The Tibetan Book of Living and Dying by Sogyal Rinpoche tells us that "spiritual care is not a luxury for a few; it is the essential right of every human being..." In Eastern cultures such as Tibet, praying for the dying and giving them spiritual care is a natural response.

121

Unfortunately, in the West, spiritual attention is primarily focused on attending the person's funeral.

In *The American Book of Living and Dying*, coauthor Richard Groves utilizes the cultural wisdom found in many books of the dead including Tibetan, Egyptian, Celtic, gnostic, and monastic, to show certain commonalities with regard to our collective human experience at the end of life. The Celtic tradition, which helped to create the hospice movement, recognized the need for a dying person to have a compassionate companion to journey with them to death's threshold. This companion was called an "anamcara" which means a soul friend. (Some may use terms such as spiritual midwife or death coach.) The anamcara made a commitment to be present with the person, to listen rather than being concerned about "doing" something, to be observant and attentive as the needs and feelings of the dying person changed, to breathe with him, to grieve with him, and to remind him he is not alone. This kind of comfort can lead to a more peaceful passage.

In the case of parents whose child is dying, the parents, too, need to know they are not alone. Oftentimes friends may avoid them in their time of need simply because they don't know what to say. As Joey and Gordy were going through the stages of Andraez's illness, they desperately needed support. The medical community certainly offered little spiritual or emotional support. Books were recommended by friends, but there was little time for reading, nor were they in the frame of mind to read books. They were caring for their children and trying to maintain normalcy as much as possible throughout their ordeal. Gordy's time was consumed with research, and as disturbing as his findings were, this gave him a sense of participation in his son's life and journey.

It is crucial that parents, as well as the children themselves, be included in decision-making. Regardless of laws that give permission to a sixteen-year-old to be a part of the decisions but deny a fifteen-and-a-half-year-old the same right, we must look at each situation case-by-case. Certainly, laws are needed to protect children from true abuse or neglect or from making unreasonable choices, but when a disease has advanced beyond reasonable hope, it must remain a human right—even for children—to die with dignity. And parents must be empowered to protect that right.

Open communication and sensitivity to the feelings and fears of a dying person, especially a dying child, is imperative. In an article titled "Silence Is Not Golden: Communicating With Children Dying From Cancer" (Journal of Clinical Oncology, Volume 23, No. 15, May 20, 2005), coauthors Estela A. Beale, Walter F. Baile, and Joann Aaron recommended a strategy for communicating effectively with terminally ill children and their families. They called it the "6 Es" strategy: (reprinted here with permission)

ESTABLISH an agreement with parents, children, and caregivers early on in the relationship with them concerning open communication. Begin by exploring the attitudes of the child's caregivers about sharing medical information with the child and answering any concerns they might have. Providing a clear explanation about the benefit of information disclosure can balance the natural tendency to be protective of the child. At the onset, it is also important to acknowledge the uncomfortable feelings that one may experience when dealing with dying children and the potential of these feelings to thwart open communication.

ENGAGE the child at the opportune time. A newly diagnosed serious illness or the occasion when a child takes a turn for the worse, are medical events that should trigger discussion. Actively attending to signs of significant behavior changes that suggest that the child is struggling with emotions will provide an opening for discussing the illness.

EXPLORE what the child already knows and wants to know about the illness. It is often surprising how much information the child already has and the extent of his or her fantasies and concerns. Exploring this will allow you to correct misperceptions and misunderstandings about the medical facts and to give information according to the child's desire for information.

EXPLAIN medical information according to the child's needs and age. Children often have many questions about what is happening and what is going to happen to them. Children may want some specific information, but not all. Asking "What would you like to know?" "What have you been worrying about?" will allow you to specifically answer specific information needs.

EMPATHIZE with the child's emotional reactions. Allowing a child to be upset and express feelings while providing physical comfort may be painful for the caregivers. Nonetheless, once emotions are vented, discussion of more concrete concerns often follows. A strategy for addressing a child's emotions includes: empathizing ("I can see that you've really been worried about this"), validating ("We've been wondering why you've been upset"), and clarifying ("Can you tell me what you've been thinking?").

ENCOURAGE the child by reassuring him or her that you will be there to listen and to be supportive. Isolation and anxiety about his or her support system and about symptoms such as pain are prime concerns for children who are dying. Acknowledging the fact that cure is not possible but that life's tasks can continue even if only in a limited way, provides some stability to the family and is perceived as a hopeful attitude. False reassurance such as saying "everything will be all right" is usually not helpful.

It is our human nature to grieve what appears to be our loss. Grieving is an important part of our healing process, and it must not be denied or avoided. There are many competent trained grief counselors that can guide a person in a healthy way through his/her process. As it says in the New Testament, Ecclesiastes 3, "to everything there is a season… a time to be born and a time to die… a time to weep and a time to laugh… a time to mourn and a time to dance…"

In the Bhagavad-Gita, Krishna advises us to not sorrow for those who have died: "The Spirit that is in all beings is immortal in them all: for the death of what cannot die, cease thou to sorrow."

So let us mourn our own sadness not the "misfortune" of one who has died, for there is an innate intelligence in every soul that knows when the time has come for its final exit. And love will lead us home. In *Home with God in a Life That Never Ends*, Neale Donald Walsch was told, "The moment you surrender to love and allow it to lead you to exactly where your soul wants to go, you will have no difficulty. All struggles then will cease, and you will know Oneness."

As our journey in this book comes to a close, I hope it will also mark a beginning. Our lives are all about beginnings and endings followed by more beginnings and more endings. Yet the ultimate truth about life is that there are no beginnings and no endings. There is only the eternal cycle of life.

We know from quantum physics that life is not static—it is constantly changing. Life is energy in motion, constantly vibrating. Whether our viewpoints stem from a spiritual faith or a scientific basis, there is one thing we can all agree on—Life is change.

Facing our fears about death and dying can help us move through the motion called "life" in a more vibrant and present way and ultimately move into our final days in a more peaceful way. In *The Tibetan Book of Living and Dying*, Sogyal Rinpoche notes that our society is primarily dedicated to the celebration of the ego, success and power, greed and ignorance. Following the path of wisdom has never been more urgent than it is now. Spiritual vision is not a luxury but vital to our very survival.

What do we really need as we approach our own death? We need to know we are not alone, that every human being, even in life's eternal nature, is impermanent in the physical world and is moving through his or her journey to completion. As I once heard someone put it in a rather blasé manner, "Some of us are checking out on the two o'clock train, some on the five o'clock, some on the ten o'clock, but we're *all* checking out!"

It's important that we be given the freedom to cry, to scream, to abreact, to emote, to talk about our fears of the unknown, and to express our fears about dying. Sogyal Rinpoche tells a story of a woman named Emily who was dying of breast cancer. Every day her daughter came to the hospice to visit her, and they seemed to enjoy a happy relationship. Yet every day when her daughter left, Emily would sit alone and cry because her daughter refused to accept the inevitability of Emily's pending death. She encouraged her mother to think positively and to pray for a cure for cancer. This meant that Emily had to put on a front and keep her fears, her thoughts, her panic, and her grief all to herself. She had no one with whom to share, with whom to explore, with whom to understand life and find meaning in death. She felt alone at a time when she most needed to be heard.

We need to know we are loved and that we are forgiven for anything we have ever done to hurt another. Likewise, it's important that we let go of any grievances we've clung to and to forgive ourselves for whatever we perceive to be our shortcomings. This is a time to review our life and feel if anything has been left undone, so we can have the completion and closure that will lead to a smooth transition. And finally, we need permission to leave, resting in the knowledge that our loved ones will be okay. Ultimately, we need to feel peace. Then can we feel anticipation. Then can we look forward as Ginny did to reuniting with loved ones who crossed over before us and to dancing among the stars. Then we can celebrate!

For many, it may be helpful to practice dying in everyday life so that when we take that final journey we will know the path to follow. A meditation or visualization practice of moving one's consciousness up from the core of the earth, through the base of the spine and up through the channel that runs along the spine, out through the crown and into a swirling tunnel of light that leads toward a distant bright light can be helpful for some. We may imagine a loved one there to greet us, or a being such as Jesus or Buddha or an angel. Whatever practice helps the dying one stay focused on a loving, peaceful destination can help quell any fears that may arise along the way. Just as Gordy had developed the guided visualization of flying unfettered throughout the cosmos to connect with the light beings that Andraez would soon be living among, a meditation or guided imagery practice can help to break the attachments to earth and loosen the bond with the physical world to make the final crossing-over more peaceful.

It is important that the dying person have a companion who will sit with him, listen to him, hold his hand or touch him lightly, breathe in unison with him, encourage him. Pray with him if requested, but refrain from projecting your own spiritual belief system on him unless you are invited to do so. This is not a time for proselytizing.

When we each face our own final moment—the moment our soul separates from the body and travels on—I believe we will find it to be the grandest, most magnificent journey we have ever imagined. Let's rejoice in our "continuation day!"

Questions for Contemplation

What is your idea of a "good death"? Describe it. How can you best prepare to have a good death?

What if you were told you had one year to live? What would you do?

What if you were told you had one month to live? What would you do?

What if you were told you had one week to live? What would you do?

What if you were told you had one day to live? What would you do?

How do you want people to remember you? Take some time to write your eulogy and/or obituary.

What would enable you to find peace as you approach your own death or a loved one's?

How best could an anamcara (spiritual guide) serve you?

Chapter Fifteen

The importance of forgiveness cannot be stressed enough. Whether we are preparing to make our transition soon or planning to live decades longer, forgiveness is crucial to our well-being and to our integrity.

It says in *A Course in Miracles*, "The Holiest place on earth is where an ancient hatred has become a present love." All of us have, at one time or another, felt like a victim. Think of all the country western he-done-me-wrong ballads! Someone did something that injured us whether physically or emotionally. Someone said something that hurt our feelings or bruised our ego. How easy it is to hold on to our grudges! We feel justified. Many of us may have harbored resentments for years without even realizing it. Perhaps we simply disconnected from our offender without ever acknowledging or expressing our feelings. We may have fussed and fumed inside until we finally stopped thinking about it and acted as if we were over it. Yet feelings of anger, resentment, frustration, indignation, or hatred may have taken up residence in our body, creating discord or even "dis-ease"

At the same time, we also may be holding on to guilt about something *we* have done, a hurt or injury we have caused another person, or perhaps a secret indiscretion we committed at some time in our life. Perhaps even a crime we got away with. Even if we have apologized and made amends to the others involved, we may still need to forgive ourselves.

Forgiveness is not about condoning or accepting what someone did. Some things that have happened to us may truly have been horrendous and may be very difficult to forgive. It may take time, and it may be necessary to seek the help of someone you trust such as a spiritual counselor, a mental health provider, or a trusted and unbiased friend or family member. It can be especially challenging to forgive someone who has not admitted to any wrong doing. But remember, forgiveness is for *you*. It's about releasing the past, so it no longer has control over you. It is a commitment to your own well-being and to your own peace of mind. Ultimately, forgiveness is a choice.

When you recognize how holding on to old resentments has affected the quality of your life, you'll be ready to let go of your role as victim. You will no longer be willing to define your life by how you've been hurt. There are many ways to help you release that murky energy of victimhood and move into a deeper compassion for your fellow human beings. Here is one process you may find effective:

Forgiveness Process:

To begin your forgiveness process, find a place where you will not be disturbed. It may be a quiet space in your home, or it may be a place in nature. Begin by centering yourself with a few slow, deep breaths. When you feel relaxed, say a prayer or do a brief meditation and invite in a Higher Power (God, an angel, a spirit guide, etc.) to assist you in this process.

Next, create in your mind a special imaginary place where you feel safe, comfortable, and inspired. It may be a special room, or it may be a natural setting such as a lofty mountaintop, a rock outcropping, a sandy beach, or a meadow filled with wild flowers. Design it in your mind, stimulating all the senses. What do you see in your special place? Are there fragrances? Sounds? Tastes? What does it feel like?

Once you have designed this place, imagine yourself sitting comfortably in the middle of it. Feel the peacefulness, the joy of being in such a beautiful setting. Feel gratitude. Call upon the spiritual presence you have invited in and ask them to guide you through this process. You are now ready to do the forgiveness work.

Invite in the Higher Self of the other person. Imagine sitting across from him, looking into his eyes. Feel the energy of your heart. This is a time to speak your truth, simply and in a heart-centered way. Don't hold anything back. Be honest about what you are thinking and feeling. Yet speak your truth with as much kindness and compassion as you can. If you are the one *asking* for forgiveness, share what is in your heart by telling the person the reason you are seeking their forgiveness.

Once you feel the process is complete, take a moment to just be with that person, feeling the energy of forgiveness flowing back and forth between you. Share your gratitude with him for being with you in this way. Thank your spiritual guides for their part in the process.

It is now time to come back into an awareness of your physical surroundings. It's important to ground yourself as you return to full consciousness by standing on the earth and imagining roots extending from your feet down into the earth. Do some stretching. Drink some water to restore your energy.

Questions for Contemplation

Are there people you feel have hurt you in any way? Are you ready to release your resentments and forgive them?

What could help you feel compassion for them?

Are there things you have done in your life over which you are harboring guilt? What would help you release your guilt and self-criticism?

Are there any other situations in your life that require closure? Closure is a process. Take your time with it.

Coming to a Close

As we bring this book to a close, remember that at the beginning of this book, we found ourselves observing a group of souls designing the Soul Plan for their upcoming time together. One by one, they came to Earth and found each other. Life was good … until fear entered their lives. Here then is the rest of their story.

The Soul Plan

Fear had entered the lives of Gordy and Joey when Andraez pushed off his oxygen mask and whispered, "Turn off my lungs." They had forgotten this part of the Soul Plan. They had forgotten the contracts they had made with one another.

Suddenly, they were frightened. How could this be happening, they demanded of an invisible god? "Why have we been forsaken?" they cried out in anguish!

Yet deep in the night, in the dreamtime, the family would gather together, and the indigo soul would remind them all of the Soul Plan. He reminded them that he would be staying with them only a few short years, that a time would come when it would appear that he would suffer, and that his earth-life would seem

133

to be cut short. That they would feel sad, angry, alone, and betrayed, that they would mourn and grieve and heal and that they would eventually grow stronger as they remembered—the Soul Plan.

The indigo one reminded Gordy, his earth-father, that there was much work still to be done, that the program he had been inspired to create, "The Secret to the Unlimited Child," now needed to be brought to completion and introduced into the world. It had been Gordy's passion and inspiration for eons. Now it would be up to him to bring it forth in the physical world. It would become Andraez's legacy.

The allotted day arrived—Andraez had fulfilled his contract. Inner eyes beholding a luminous presence that reached for him, he sent silent goodbyes through his heart to his loved ones. With his frail voice, he asked to be set free. "Turn off my lungs." He knew the love that flowed through his family, binding them together eternally, would live on. He knew that he would live on.

Hearing the soft, compelling melody of distant wind chimes, he felt himself being drawn into a tunnel. There was a light so brilliant his earth-eyes could not withstand it, but his soul-eyes could not resist its pull. Home! He was going home! He would wait for the others there. He would be with them from that faraway place, unseen. Loving them … always … all ways.

And one day, they would all be together once again, in that timeless, spaceless void between lifetimes. They would celebrate their accomplishments, and they would plan their next journey.

And so it was.

Dear Reader,

I invite you to consider that not only was Andraez's life and death part of the Soul Plan, but indeed, my writing of this book and your reading it has concluded this part of the plan. Thank you for joining us on this journey.

Donna Corso

THE END

or perhaps

THE BEGINNING

Death is not extinguishing the Light; It is putting out the lamp because the dawn has come.

—Rabindranath Tagore

In Loving Memory of Andraez Diego Lee
June 30, 1995–March 31, 2003

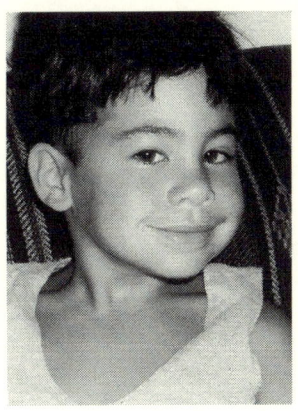

If Tears Could Build a Stairway
(author unknown)

If tears could build a stairway
And memories were a lane
We would walk right up to Heaven
And bring you back again

No farewell words were spoken
No time to say goodbye
You were gone before we knew it
And only God knows why

Our hearts still ache in sadness
And secret tears still flow
What it meant to lose you
No one will ever know

But know we know you want us
To mourn for you no more
To remember all the happy times
Life still has much in store

Since you'll never be forgotten
We pledge to you today
A hallowed place within our hearts
Is where you'll always stay

137

READERS' COMMENTS

This book took me totally by surprise. The surprise was: I didn't expect to love it so much.

Donna Corso has crafted a story about how we love each other. How, in spite of the phenomenal adversity in this family's life, they loved each other.

Sure. It might've been easy to take shots at the medical or pharmaceutical industries. It's easy to do. Donna resisted that temptation and instead brought us in close to a tender pace—a helplessly human place and made this book about love. And in this way, Donna's writing is infused with a tenderness that is at once fiercely strong and endlessly compassionate.

I reread the first few lines of the book and was hooked … all over again. Tears welled in my eyes. Because this book reminds me of how much in love I am with the way we love each other. Institutions, governments, and politics are dwarfed by the enormity of the human spirit when we stand undaunted, fearless, and united in love.

Michael Mish
Composer/writer

When the Wind Chimes Chime is a very powerful book. I blasted through the pages of this poignant story (the first part of the book) which plays the vehicle for opening one's heart to the point of raw vulnerability. This opening begs the reader to continue on with the second part of the book so that we are really able to hear and absorb that fear need *not* be inextricably connected to the experience of death. This is one of those books that stay with you long after the last sentence has been read. I will recommend this book to many.

Nannette Rogers-Kennedy
Humanity's Team

Addendum A

The Secret to the Unlimited Child™

A Children's Life Empowerment Program

Life Mastery Unlimited, LLC has created **The Secret to the Unlimited Child™** out of the calling of many parents, educators and employers who have witnessed a "significant adverse shift" within the youth of our country. The purpose of this program is to assist as many of those as possible who are in positions of great influence on our youth, primarily parents, by offering them a life empowering tool that will promote a higher quality of life for the children and family.

Lifelong benefits for your child include:

Self-Esteem	Focus and Concentration
Courage	Confidence
Kindness and Giving	Honor
Compassion	Respect
Discipline	Forgiveness
Self-Management	Manifesting
Self-Love	Stewardship of Nature
Creativity	Connecting with Higher Power
Parent–Child Communication.	Discovering True Happiness
Ambition/Motivation	

The Secret to The Unlimited Child™ is an audio CD program designed to facilitate the development of a positive internal belief system in children using one of the most effective, proven, positive reinforcement techniques known today—affirmations. Powerful affirming statements synergistically combined with 60-beat-per-minute music has been discovered to assist the mind in absorbing the content. The affirmations are softly audible, then gradually fade beneath the music as the child enters the sleep state. There is also an upbeat "daytime" CD titled "Hour of Power." This impactful CD library also includes a guide and workbook for parents.

FOR MORE INFORMATION VISIT
The Secret to the Unlimited Child™.
http://www.theunlimitedchild.com/

Gordy Lee

Addendum B

California Citizens for Health Freedom
About the Legislation
Integrative Treatment of Cancer Bill

The Integrative Treatment of this Cancer Bill is groundbreaking legislation. Currently, physicians across the US are limited to treating cancer with only radiation, chemotherapy or surgery, or they run the very real risk of losing their medical license. Over the last few decades, research has shown success in using natural and nontoxic approaches to treating cancer which have gone unnoticed by most of mainstream medicine because of the lack of funding to support large studies of substances and approaches that cannot be patented.

This bill will change this paradigm in cancer by protecting physicians who want to provide medicines and treatments that have research supporting their use. The bill includes strong provisions that protect the public by ensuring the patient is well informed about the treatment the doctor is providing as well as provisions to regularly measure the progress of their treatments.

It also limits cancer treatments for reducing the size of a cancer, slowing the growth of a cancer, or improving the quality of life of a cancer patient. This approach opens the door for individual doctors, hospitals, and research institutions to study a wide variety of treatments that are expected to result in new cancer cures but limit treatment goals by respecting concerns about exaggerated claims of curing cancer without more in depth research.

What does this bill accomplish?

It makes the decision on how to treat cancer a private decision between the doctor and his or her patient. It stops medical boards from disciplining doctors for providing integrative cancer treatments and opens the door for advancements in medicine.

It protects the public by making sure patients are well informed during the course of their care and that doctors follow strict regulations. It encourages coordination of care between the doctor providing integrative cancer care and the doctors providing conventional cancer care.

Who benefits from the Integrative Treatment of Cancer?
Patients will have access to more holistic approaches that show promise in the treatment of cancer and will no longer need to travel to Mexico, overseas, or out of state for integrative cancer treatment. Doctors, hospitals and research institutions will be provided a "safe harbor" where they can study a wide variety of safe and effective approaches in treatment of cancer patients. The State of California will become a leader in integrative cancer treatments, become a destination in the US for care, and benefit financially from the influx of patients and clinics that will specialize in the integrative treatment of cancer. Manufacturers of high-quality nutriceuticals, intravenous therapies, and other substances and therapies that show promise in the treatment of cancer, in peer-reviewed and scientific journals.

About the California Citizens for Health Freedom
The California Citizens for Health Freedom (CCHF) is a 501(c)4 nonprofit organization whose mission is to protect and expand the right of citizens to have access to alternative medicine, natural treatments, natural nutritional products and to have a toxic free environment. Their funding comes from donations (pledges) from citizens and some physicians. As a citizen's based organization they depend upon our support and help.

California Citizens for Health Freedom
2362 Palermo Road, Palermo, CA 95968
E-Mail: freedom@citizenshealth.org

Donna Corso is a Reiki master, a certified hypnotherapist and an ordained interfaith minister. Believing that Life is eternal, and that what we call "death" is simply Life continuing in a different form, she encourages people to heal and release their fear of dying, to embrace Life more fully while in this physical world, and to move forward gracefully into the spiritual realm at the time of their soul's choosing.

Donna resides in Ashland, Oregon, where she has been personal assistant to author Neale Donald Walsch since 2001.

3982703R00088

Printed in Great Britain
by Amazon.co.uk, Ltd.,
Marston Gate.